RESEARCH MADE EASY

Exploring Positivist and Post-positivist Approaches

Anna Tierney

RePrac LTD T/A Online Therapy NZ

CONTENTS

Perspectives

Copyright

ISBN:

979-8-89778-126-3

Publisher:

RePrac Lt TA Online Therapy NZ

Contact Information: info@onlinetherapy.co.nz

Publisher Contact information: anna@reprac.co.nz

DEDICATION

I started writing this book at the beginning of my research career. My first major research project was during my fourth year at university. At that time, I was still exploring the concepts of positivism and post-positivism, which is why I wrote this book and want to dedicate it to students starting their research journeys. It aims to help them expand their understanding of the world through research methods that allow them to contribute to the knowledge of society. This work highlights the importance of curiosity and the ongoing quest for knowledge, which help shape our understanding of ourselves, our communities, and the world around us.

This dedication also includes the wider community of scholars who continuously develop and refine research methodologies. Their insights and contributions are crucial for progress in the social sciences and beyond. Additionally, I recognise those who challenge established ideas and encourage thoughtful discussions, leading to deeper and more comprehensive understandings of complex social issues. Their contributions are key to promoting critical thinking, healthy debates, and ultimately, a more informed world.

I also want to dedicate this book to my son, Kyle, who has supported me throughout my studies by editing my work and helping me brainstorm ideas. A special thanks go to my husband, Philip, for believing in my abilities and encouraging me to pursue my dreams and to my friends who assisted in the editing process.

PREFACE

A nna's career as a counsellor began in 2004 when she volunteered to support children living with HIV, igniting her passion for helping others. In 2017, she launched Online Therapy in New Zealand to meet the growing demand for accessible mental health support for adults. With a diverse background in various therapeutic approaches, Anna emphasises the importance of building strong therapeutic relationships and creating a safe space for individuals to explore their challenges.

In 2024, Anna relocated to the UK, bringing her rich insights and experiences with her. As this book delves into research methodologies, her dedication to mental health informs her perspective, encouraging readers to consider how research can drive meaningful change in the field of therapy and beyond.

This book addresses a critical gap in social science research by emphasising the role of philosophical foundations. The choice between positivist and post-positivist perspectives extends beyond technical details; it significantly shapes research questions, methodologies, and interpretations. Initially, Anna found research challenging, struggling with complex terms and concepts that felt overwhelming. This experience inspired her to write this book, aiming to make research methods and terminology more accessible and easier to grasp for readers.

While many resources focus on specific research methods, few offer an accessible yet rigorous examination of the core philosophical distinctions between these paradigms. This volume fills that gap by clearly analysing positivism and post-positivism, highlighting their key differences in research paradigms, ontology, epistemology, and methodology.

Through engaging case studies and real-world examples, this book illustrates the practical implications of selecting a research paradigm, empowering beginner students with a solid understanding of these concepts. It enables them to make informed choices in their research, proving particularly suited for newcomers while also offering valuable insights for graduate students, refining their methodological understanding.

Furthermore, this book encourages critical self-reflection, prompting readers to examine the assumptions behind their research and the impact of their chosen perspectives. The goal is to foster intellectual integrity and self-awareness throughout the research process. By carefully considering these foundational philosophical issues, researchers can enhance the rigour and trustworthiness of their work, leading to more meaningful outcomes.

INTRODUCTION

The social sciences encompass diverse approaches to understanding the complexities of human behaviour and society. At the core of this exploration are the contrasting paradigms of positivism and post-positivism, which profoundly influence how researchers approach inquiry. This book investigates these paradigms, detailing their fundamental principles, key differences, and implications for research design and interpretation.

Positivism is defined as an evidence-based approach grounded in the belief in an objective reality that can be measured through systematic observation and empirical testing. In contrast, post-positivism acknowledges the role of human perception and the subjective nature of knowledge that emerges from lived experiences.

The book examines the central philosophical distinctions between these paradigms, focusing on their ontological (nature of reality), epistemological (nature of knowledge), and methodological (research approaches) foundations. A balanced assessment of the strengths and weaknesses of each paradigm highlights the importance of aligning methodologies with philosophical assumptions.

Through practical examples, case studies, and real-world applications, Anna illustrates the use of positivist (quantitative focus) and post-positivist (contextual and interpretative) research designs. Additionally, she explores specific movements within post-positivism, such as constructivism (knowledge as co-created through interaction) and critical realism (CR)—a philosophical approach that distinguishes between the real and observable worlds, often used in the social sciences—and their contributions to understanding social phenomena.

This text also emphasises the significance of recognising researcher bias and contextual factors, as well as the necessity for transparent and ethical research practices. Ultimately, Anna aims to equip researchers with the tools to critically evaluate their approaches, fostering more rigorous, valid, and impactful contributions to the social sciences. By making these complex concepts more accessible, she seeks to empower readers, just as she wished to do in her own journey of understanding research.

CHAPTER 1: UNDERSTANDING POSITIVISM AND POST-POSITIVISM

INTRODUCING POSITIVISM

Positivism's foundational pillar is the belief that knowledge arises primarily from observation and empirical methods (evidence-based approaches) (De Vos, Strydom, Fouche, & Delport, 2005). This perspective asserts that a proper understanding of the world requires tangible, sensory-driven evidence rather than abstract reasoning or speculation (Dawadi, Shrestha, & Giri, 2021). At its core, positivism emphasises an objective reality that exists independently of the observer. This reality is governed by natural laws that can be discovered through systematic observation and scientific inquiry ("Positivism | Definition, History, Theories, & Criticism | Britannica," n.d.).

Central to the positivist perspective is the idea that knowledge should focus on identifying causal relationships (cause and effect) between variables. This commitment to empirical evidence necessitates the use of quantitative methods (numerical data), favouring measurable information and statistical analysis to test hypotheses (testable predictions) and draw general conclusions (Maksimović & Evtimov, 2023). Correlational studies are also essential to quantitative research and positivism as they objectively assess relationships between variables, helping predict outcomes and generate hypotheses, but do not imply causation.

A key feature of positivist research is its emphasis on objectivity. Researchers are expected to remain neutral and minimise the influence of personal biases and subjective interpretations on the research process (Maksimović & Evtimov, 2023).

This pursuit of objectivity requires careful design and execution of studies, using controlled methods to ensure replicability (the ability to repeat the study) (Sovacool, Axsen, & Sorrell, 2018).

Deductive reasoning (starting with general principles and testing them) is essential to the positivist approach. Researchers develop hypotheses based on established theories and then test them through observation (De Vos et al., 2005). If the data supports these hypotheses, the theory is strengthened; if not, the theory may need to be revised or rejected. This hypothesis development, testing, and refinement process is critical for gaining a more accurate understanding of reality (Casula, Rangarajan, & Shields, 2021).

The preference for quantitative data in positivist research stems from its focus on objectivity and measurability. Quantitative data, usually in numerical form, allows researchers to identify patterns and relationships between variables. Common quantitative methods include surveys, experiments, and statistical analyses like regression analysis, analysis of variance (ANOVA), and t-tests (Kim, 2014a).

Positivism Example

To illustrate positivism, let's consider a hypothetical example in research in the social sciences. A researcher exploring the link between socioeconomic status (SES) and educational achievement may use a large-scale survey to collect data.

Below is a hypothetical example of how the data could be organised (Maksimović & Evtimov, 2023):

Table 1: Hypothetical Example of data organisation

Stude nt ID	Income Level	Parental Education Level	Acade mic Performa nce (GPA)
1	Low	High School	2.5
2	Medium	Bachelor's Degree	3.2
3	High	Graduate Degree	3.9
4	Low	High School	2.7
5	Medium	Some College	3.0
6	High	Bachelor's Degree	3.8

The data set includes six students with varying income levels and parental education backgrounds. Each student's academic performance is quantified in terms of their GPA (Grade Point Average), allowing for objective analysis. The researcher could examine the relationships between these factors by analysing this quantitative data using statistical methods like regression analysis, which estimates the relationship between a dependent variable (the outcome) and one or more independent variables (the predictors) to make predictions. The focus would be on identifying significant relationships and drawing general conclusions about how socioeconomic status affects educational achievement across different populations.

Income Level: Based on the data, students with higher income levels (Students 3 and 6) appear to have higher GPAs (3.9 and 3.8) compared to their low income counterparts (Students 1 and 4) with GPAs of 2.5 and 2.7. This suggests a potential positive relationship between income level and academic performance, confirming the hypothesis.

Parental Education: Similarly, the table indicates that students with parents who have higher educational attainment—specifically, those whose parents hold a Bachelor's or Graduate Degree—are also performing better academically. For example, Students 2 and 3, whose parents have higher education, show GPAs of 3.2 and 3.9, while those with parents who completed only high school (Students 1 and 4) have lower GPAs.

The findings from this hypothetical analysis could lead the researcher to conclude that both income level and parental education are significant predictors of academic performance among students. The statistical evidence gathered would allow the researcher to begin to identify causal relationships, providing insights into how socioeconomic factors influence educational outcomes.

The strength of positivism in this context lies in its ability to generate **generalisable laws** across different populations by using large-scale surveys, allowing for the findings to be applied in educational policy-making. However, the researcher should also be cautious of potential confounding factors, such as differing levels of student motivation or school resources, which could skew results.

Another example is in political science. Researchers could study how campaign advertising affects voter turnout by conducting a controlled experiment. Below is another hypothetical table representing the data collected from participants exposed to different types of campaign advertisements:

Table 2 Hypothetical Example of a controlled experiment

Participant ID	Ad Type	Group	Voter Turnout (Yes/No)
1	Informative	Group A	Yes
2	Emotional Appeal	Group B	Yes
3	Negative Ad	Group C	No
4	Informative	Group A	Yes
5	Emotional Appeal	Group B	Yes
6	Negative Ad	Group C	No

In this table, participants are assigned to different groups based on the type of advertisement they are exposed to: informative, emotional appeal, or negative advertisements. Researchers can compare the voter turnout rates across the different groups to assess the effectiveness of each advertising strategy.

The analysis would focus on identifying significant differences in turnout, helping to understand how different types of ads influence voter behaviour. The researchers can analyse the voter turnout rates among the different groups. The expected outcomes from the table indicate that:

Informative Ads (Group A): Participants in this group show a high turnout (100%—both participants turned out to vote).

Emotional Appeal Ads (Group B): This group also has a high turnout (100%), suggesting that emotional messaging may effectively engage voters.

Negative Ads (Group C): In contrast, participants in Group C show no turnout (0%). This finding may point to a lack of motivation or negative feelings resulting from exposure to negative advertising, which could discourage participation.

The analysis focuses on identifying significant differences in voter turnout across the groups, allowing researchers to draw conclusions about the effectiveness of different advertising strategies. For example, the significant turnout in Groups A and B suggests that informative and emotional appeal ads are more effective at engaging voters than negative ads.

The lack of turnout in Group C illustrates that negative advertising may have adverse effects on voter engagement.

This kind of experiment highlights objective measurement

and statistical analysis to consider causal relationships. By employing controlled experiments and analysing turnout data, researchers can provide valuable insights that inform campaign strategies and contribute to understanding voter behaviour in the political arena.

Fields Embracing a Positivist Paradigm

Positivism is vital in research methodology, especially in fields reliant on quantifiable data and statistical analysis. Professions such as natural sciences, engineering, medicine, social sciences, data science, quality control, and environmental science depend on empirical evidence and scientific methods (De Vos et al., 2005). These fields use quantitative research and statistical analysis to derive conclusions. Positivism's focus on objectivity and rigorous methods has led to substantial advancements in various disciplines (Horowitz, 2004).

Limitations of Positivism

However, the quest for objectivity in positivism does face challenges (De Vos et al., 2005). Critics argue that removing all subjectivity is unrealistic, as researchers' biases and values can affect all stages of research, from question formulation to data interpretation (Horowitz, 2004). Additionally, focusing solely on quantifiable data may oversimplify complex social phenomena that are difficult to capture numerically. Important qualitative aspects of human experience and social interactions may be overlooked (Delmas & Giles, 2022).

INTRODUCING POST-POSITIVISM

Post-positivism arises as a critical response to positivism, addressing its core assumptions, particularly the ideas of absolute objectivity (complete impartiality) and the belief that researchers can completely separate themselves from the subjects they study in social phenomena (human behaviour and social interactions) (Buchanan, 1998). While post-positivism acknowledges the value of empirical evidence (information gained through observation and experience) and rigorous methodology (systematic approaches to research), it critiques the notion of an entirely objective reality (De Vos et al., 2005).

A significant limitation of positivism is its assumption of value neutrality (the idea that research can be free of biases). Although positivist research aims for objectivity, complete separation from biases and personal beliefs is virtually impossible (Hammersley, 2017). Researchers inherently bring their own backgrounds and experiences into the research process, influencing every stage from question formulation to data interpretation (De Vos et al., 2005). For instance, a study evaluating the effectiveness of a social programme may unintentionally favour certain outcomes if the researcher holds strong beliefs about its efficacy (effectiveness). These subtle biases can affect data collection and interpretation, leading to results that do not accurately reflect social reality.

Moreover, the focus on quantifiable data (measurable information) in positivist research often overlooks the richness of qualitative insights (non-numerical information that provides context) (Bazen, Barg, & Takeshita, 2021). While quantitative methods are essential for identifying trends within large datasets, they can fail to capture the complexities of human experiences (Smirnov, 2024). For example, examining social inequalities through income data alone may miss the nuanced experiences of individuals facing discrimination (unfair treatment) or systemic barriers (deep-rooted obstacles). Qualitative methods, such as interviews and ethnographic observations (in-depth studies of people in their natural environments), are vital for understanding the context and individual perspectives that shape social realities.

Positivism's pursuit of generalisable findings (results that apply broadly) may also neglect the importance of context. The idea that research results can universally apply disregards social phenomena' variability (differences) (De Vos et al., 2005). For instance, an effective educational intervention in one cultural context (setting) may not yield similar results in another. Post-positivism recognises this context-dependence and asserts that social realities are influenced by a complex interplay (interaction) of factors.

In addition, the deterministic view of causality (the idea that one thing directly causes another) inherent in positivism simplifies the relationship between variables (elements being studied), assuming straightforward cause-and-effect connections (E. K. Chen, 2024). However, social phenomena are often marked by intricate interactions (complex relationships) and emergent properties (new characteristics that arise from these interactions) that resist simple explanations. Post-positivism embraces a more nuanced understanding of causality, acknowledging the roles of chance, context, and various influencing factors (De Vos et al., 2005).

The issue of the observer effect (when the act of observation changes what is being observed) also challenges the positivist claim to objectivity. The act of observation can influence the behaviour of individuals being studied. For example, classroom dynamics may shift if students know they are being observed. Post-positivism emphasises reflexivity (the researcher's self-awareness), urging researchers to be aware of their influence on the research process (Parsons, 1974).

Overall, post-positivism offers a more comprehensive framework for understanding social reality. It critiques the pursuit of absolute objectivity in positivism and acknowledges the potential for researcher bias and context dependence in knowledge production. By accepting this complexity, post-positivism advocates for a more reflexive research approach that values multiple interpretations and perspectives (Maksimović & Evtimov, 2023).

This paradigm encourages transparency (openness) in acknowledging assumptions, biases, and methodological choices. It highlights the importance of triangulation—using various methods and data sources to cross-validate findings (De Vos et al., 2005). For example, examining the impact of social media on political polarisation (the division of people into opposing groups) could involve both quantitative analyses and qualitative interviews, creating a more layered (detailed) understanding of the issue (a mixed methods approach).

Adding to this, **crystallisation** allows researchers to view data from different angles, enriching the research findings. By considering various perspectives, researchers can uncover deeper insights that could otherwise remain hidden (Ellingson, 2017).

For example, in studying social media impacts, crystallisation encourages examining the interplay between quantitative data and qualitative narratives to provide a fuller picture of how social media shapes political beliefs.

Table 3: Mixed Methods Overview Example Application

Method	Description	Purpose
Quantitative Survey	Surveys distributed to a diverse sample.	To collect numerical data and identify patterns.
Data Analysis	Statistical methods (e.g., regression analysis) used to analyse survey results.	To establish correlations and trends among variables.
Qualitative Interviews	In-depth interviews with a subset of survey participants to explore their experiences.	To gain deeper insights and analyse themes that occur.
Triangulation	Both quantitative and qualitative methods were used to cross-validate findings.	To provide a more comprehensive understanding.
Crystallisation	Examining data from multiple perspectives to enrich interpretations and reveal deeper insights.	To enhance the depth and nuance of understanding in the research findings.

In summary of the example above:

Research Topic: Impact of Social Media on Political Polarisation

Triangulation Purpose: Combining quantitative analysis of survey data and qualitative insights from interviews to create a detailed understanding of how social media shapes political beliefs.

Crystallisation Purpose: Exploring the data through various lenses —including the narratives from interviews and the statistical trends —enables the researcher to uncover richer insights into how social media influences political identity and engagement across different demographic groups.

Integrating qualitative and quantitative methods enriches understanding of social phenomena, combining the breadth provided by quantitative data with the depth of qualitative insights (De Vos et al., 2005). Acknowledging limitations within the post-positivist framework leads to a more cautious and reflexive approach, valuing ongoing questioning and critical evaluation. Rather than seeking definitive answers, post-positivist research aims for tentative explanations (provisional understandings) and recognises that knowledge is constantly evolving and open to revision (Dawadi et al., 2021).

This contrasts with positivism's more definite belief in unquestionable truths, fostering a collaborative process in knowledge production that embraces dialogue (discussion) and refinement of understanding (Cohen, Manion, & Morrison, 2018). By acknowledging the inherent uncertainties in social inquiry, post-positivism promotes a responsible and nuanced approach to the complexities of human experience, ultimately advancing a richer understanding of social phenomena (De Vos et al., 2005).

Fields Embracing a Post-Positivist Design

In the **social sciences**, disciplines such as sociology, anthropology, and psychology apply post-positivist methods to understand the intricacies of human behaviour and social contexts, accommodating subjective experiences. In **education**, post-positivism is employed to investigate teaching practices and learning environments while considering multiple perspectives and contextual factors. The **health sciences**, including nursing and public health, utilise post-positivist approaches to assess how social, economic, and cultural influences affect health outcomes. In **environmental studies**, researchers combine qualitative and quantitative methods to explore human-environment interactions, acknowledging the subjective nature of ecological issues.

In **management and organisational studies**, post-positivist designs help uncover complexities in organisational behaviour and culture. Finally, **cultural studies** leverage post-positivism to analyse meanings and interpretations of cultural phenomena through qualitative methods.

Limitations of Post-positivism

Post-positivist research has several significant limitations that should be considered. While post-positivists believe that truth exists, they acknowledge that we can only understand it imperfectly. This belief leads researchers to constantly seek more information, question their own biases, and explore different viewpoints. On the extreme end, post-positivism may not fully capture the intricate nature of social realities by only prioritising observable facts. Therefore, while post-positivism provides valuable insights, researchers should recognise its limitations and use various research methods to understand complex social issues fully.

UNDERSTANDING ONTOLOGY, EPISTEMOLOGY, AND METHODOLOGY IN POSITIVISM AND POST-POSITIVISM

To grasp the main ideas of positivism and post-positivism, it's essential to look at their basic beliefs about three important areas (Shannon-Baker, 2023):

Ontology (what kind of reality exists and how we define it), **Epistemology** (how we acquire knowledge and what we consider to be knowledge), and **Methodology** (the methods and approaches we use to conduct research).

Understanding these areas helps clarify how each paradigm views the world and influences research practices. These interconnected elements form the philosophical foundation of each approach, shaping research questions, methods, and interpretations of findings (Cohen et al., 2018). While both paradigms aim to generate knowledge, they differ significantly regarding the nature of reality (ontology), the relationship between the knower (the person seeking knowledge) and the known (the knowledge itself) (epistemology), and the appropriate methods for acquiring knowledge (methodology) (De Vos et al., 2005).

Starting with ontology, the study of being or existence, positivism embraces a **realist ontology** (belief in a single, unchanging reality), asserting that a single, objective reality exists independently of the observer (Gabriel, 2015). This reality, governed by natural laws (universal principles that describe how the world works), can be discovered through scientific inquiry (systematic investigation). In the positivist view, the social world operates according to predictable patterns and causal relationships (cause and effect). Therefore, social science research aims to uncover these underlying laws and establish **generalisable principles** (rules that apply across different situations) (Sovacool et al., 2018). For example, a positivist researcher studying poverty may focus on quantifiable indicators (measurable signs) such as income levels and housing conditions to establish correlations (relationships between two or more factors) across different populations. This approach assumes that these measurable factors represent a true and stable reality.

In contrast, post-positivism adopts a **critical realist ontology** (understanding that while a real world exists, our perception of it is limited). It acknowledges an objective reality while recognising the limitations of human perception (how we understand and interpret the world) (Shannon-Baker, 2023). Post-positivists argue that understanding reality is inherently partial (not complete) and shaped by perspectives, values, and experiences. This implies that there is not one single truth; rather, multiple interpretations shaped by social contexts (the environment that influences people) exist (De Vos et al., 2005). This holistic perspective is akin to Gestalt principles, which emphasise that the whole is greater than the sum of its parts, urging researchers to consider the broader context in which phenomena occur. For instance, a post-positivist studying poverty may incorporate qualitative methods (non-numerical approaches) like interviews to explore the lived experiences of individuals facing economic hardship, recognising that poverty involves complex social dynamics (interconnected factors) beyond mere quantifiable metrics.

The epistemological positions (theories about how we know what we know) of positivism and post-positivism further distinguish them. Positivism adheres to an **objectivist epistemology** (belief in obtaining knowledge independent of personal biases), emphasising the possibility of obtaining objective knowledge detached from researcher biases (Shannon-Baker, 2023). Knowledge is seen as accumulated through empirical observation (information gained through experience, such as observation or experimentation), with the researcher acting as a neutral observer (someone who does not influence outcomes) (De Vos et al., 2005). In this model, rigorous methods aim to minimise bias and ensure objectivity. However, achieving complete objectivity is often challenging, and the ideal of value-free research (research that is not influenced by personal beliefs) is seldom fully realised (Shannon-Baker, 2023).

Conversely, post-positivism embraces a **subjectivist or constructivist epistemology** (personal experiences and social contexts shape knowledge), recognising that knowledge is constructed within specific contexts and influenced by the researcher's values and beliefs (Sovacool et al., 2018). While it appreciates objectivity as a goal, post-positivism emphasises the importance of acknowledging subjectivity (the influence of personal feelings and opinions) and the provisional nature of knowledge claims (acknowledging that knowledge is subject to change). This perspective promotes **reflexivity** (self-awareness), encouraging researchers to critically reflect on their positionality (how their identity and experiences influence research) and how it impacts the research (Busetto, Wick, & Gumbinger, 2020). Acknowledging multiple perspectives enriches understanding complex social phenomena without negating the pursuit of knowledge (Busetto et al., 2020).

Finally, methodological differences (how research is conducted) between positivism and post-positivism arise from their ontological and epistemological assumptions. Positivism favours **quantitative methods** (approaches that focus on numerical data), utilising surveys, experiments, and statistical analyses (mathematical methods to understand data) to measure variables (elements being studied), identify correlations, and test causal hypotheses (proposed explanations). This emphasis on large-scale data collection often results in a less detailed understanding of specific contexts (De Vos et al., 2005).

On the other hand, post-positivism embraces a more diverse range of methods, incorporating both **quantitative and qualitative approaches** (methods that explore non-numerical data, like text or interviews).This promotes **methodological pluralism** to gain a more comprehensive understanding of social phenomena. Qualitative methods, such as interviews, ethnography (in-depth study of people in their natural settings), and discourse analysis (study of communication), allow researchers to explore the complexities of social phenomena in greater depth. **Mixed-methods designs**, which combine quantitative and qualitative approaches, provide a more holistic (complete and well-rounded) understanding of research problems. For example, an investigation into the impact of a new educational policy could measure changes in student test scores quantitatively while also exploring the experiences of students and teachers affected by the policy qualitatively (Dawadi et al., 2021).

Table 4: Comparing Ontology, Epistemology, and Methodology

Concept	Positivism	Post-positivism
Ontology	**Realist Ontology -** Belief in a single, unchanging reality that exists independently of the observer.	**Critical Realist Ontology -** Acknowledges an objective reality while recognising the limitations of human perception.
Methodology Focus	Emphasis on quantitative methods (measurable data) to uncover laws and generalisable principles.	Utilises both quantitative and qualitative approaches to develop nuanced and context-specific understandings.
Epistemology	**Objectivist Epistemology -** Knowledge is obtained through empirical observation	**Subjectivist/ Constructivist Epistemology -** Knowledge is constructed within specific contexts, shaped by the researcher's values and beliefs. Recognises subjectivity.
Methodological Approaches	Quantitative methods, employing surveys, experiments, and statistical analysis	Embraces a diverse range of methods, including qualitative methods.

In summary, the fundamental differences between positivism and post-positivism lie in their views of reality, the researcher's role, and preferred methods for acquiring knowledge. Positivism seeks universal laws and generalisable principles through quantitative inquiry, while post-positivism embraces critical realism and utilises various methods to develop nuanced and context-specific understandings of social phenomena. Understanding these core differences enables researchers to make informed choices about their theoretical frameworks and methodologies, ultimately enhancing the rigour and relevance of social science research.

PARADIGM SHIFTS AND THEIR IMPLICATIONS FOR RESEARCH

B uilding on our understanding of the differences between positivism and post-positivism, it is crucial to explore how adopting either approach significantly impacts the research process. Choosing a paradigm is not merely a matter of preference; it shapes the entire research journey in impactful ways.

Research Questions

For example, consider two researchers investigating the same broad topic: the impact of social media on adolescent mental health. A positivist researcher may frame a question like, *"What is the statistical relationship between time spent on social media and levels of anxiety in adolescents?"* This question reflects a positivist commitment to quantifiable variables and objective measurement.

In contrast, a post-positivist may ask, *"How do adolescents perceive their experiences with social media in relation to their mental wellbeing?"* Here, the focus shifts to understanding the subjective experiences of individuals, acknowledging that multiple interpretations exist. This difference in framing guides the type of research conducted and reflects deeper philosophical beliefs about knowledge and reality.

Study Design

The choice of paradigm influences the research design as well. The positivist researcher would likely opt for a structured study involving a large sample, using surveys or experiments to gather numerical data. For example, they may conduct a survey where hundreds of adolescents rate their social media usage and anxiety levels, allowing for statistical analysis that seeks to establish clear correlations. Meanwhile, the post-positivist researcher would design a more flexible study that allows for deeper exploration (Busetto et al., 2020). They may conduct in-depth interviews with a smaller group of adolescents, asking open-ended questions about their experiences with social media (Dawadi et al., 2021). For instance, these interviews could reveal that some teens use social media for support and connection, while others feel it increases feelings of isolation. This design captures the complex reality of how social media is experienced differently by individuals.

Data Collection Techniques

The methods used to gather information further illustrate the contrasts between these paradigms. A positivist approach relies on structured instruments, such as questionnaires with fixed response choices, providing consistency across a large population. This method helps ensure data can be statistically analysed, yielding generalisable findings (Cohen et al., 2018).

On the other hand, a post-positivist approach uses qualitative techniques like interviews or focus groups. Researchers can discuss participants' feelings and thoughts regarding social media during these sessions (De Vos et al., 2005). For example, a researcher may ask one adolescent how their online interactions make them feel. The depth of such qualitative data allows researchers to uncover rich narratives highlighting the intricate relationships between social media use and mental health.

Interpretation of Findings

Finally, how research findings are interpreted and communicated differs significantly between positivism and post-positivism. The positivist researcher may be more included to be present results as objective truths, often focusing on statistical significance and reporting measurable effects. This could lead to statements like, *"There is a statistically significant correlation between high social media usage and increased anxiety levels in adolescents,"* suggesting a universal conclusion applicable to all adolescents.

In contrast, the post-positivist researcher would interpret their findings as one of many possible understandings. They may say, *"Participants expressed varied experiences with social media that contribute to feelings of anxiety, highlighting the need to consider individual circumstances.*" This interpretation emphasises that findings cannot be universally applied and should be understood within specific contexts.These implications extend throughout every research project stage and affect its quality. When evaluating the quality of research, three fundamental concepts come into play: validity, reliability, and generalisability. Understanding these terms is crucial for conducting robust research and accurately interpreting findings.

Validity refers to the accuracy of the research findings—whether the results truly reflect the phenomenon being studied (Patino & Ferreira, 2018). *Example:* Consider a study to assess the effectiveness of a new therapy for anxiety. If the study uses a well-validated anxiety scale to measure participants' anxiety levels before and after treatment, then the findings are likely to be valid. However, if the researchers relied on informal self-reports that were not systematically assessed, the validity of their conclusions could be compromised. Researchers must ensure that their measures accurately capture what they intend to study, which often involves careful selection of instruments and questioning methods.

Reliability refers to the consistency of results across different studies and settings. It ensures that if the research were repeated, the outcomes would be similar, assuming nothing else has changed (Heale & Twycross, 2015).*Example:* If a study measuring the effectiveness of a new educational programme yields consistent improvements in student performance when repeated in several schools, it indicates high reliability. Conversely, if the findings vary widely when the research is conducted again, this raises questions about the reliability of the results. Researchers can enhance reliability by employing standardised procedures, ensuring data collection methods are consistently applied across participants.

Generalisability is the extent to which findings from a study can be applied to broader contexts beyond the specific sample being investigated. It addresses the question of whether the results can be assumed to hold true for other groups (Tiokhin, Hackman, Munira, Jesmin, & Hruschka, 2019). *Example:* If a study on social media use is conducted solely with urban teenagers, the findings could not generalise to rural adolescents or adults who use social media differently. To enhance generalisability, researchers should ensure their sample adequately represents the larger population. This could involve using random sampling techniques to select participants from diverse backgrounds, ensuring wider applicability of the results.

Researchers typically design large-scale surveys and experiments in a positivist approach, which emphasises objective reality and quantifiable data (Cohen et al., 2018). For example, consider a researcher studying the connection between socioeconomic status (SES) and educational attainment. They could utilise the following strategies:

Quantitative Methods: The researcher could conduct a large-scale quantitative study, employing statistical techniques like regression analysis (De Vos et al., 2005). This method examines how changes in SES relate to variations in educational outcomes, allowing the researcher to test specific hypotheses about the interaction between these variables (Maksimović & Evtimov, 2023).

Objective Measurements: In striving for accuracy, the researcher focuses on obtaining precise data, such as test scores and family income. They aim to minimise researcher bias to ensure their findings can be reliably replicated and generalised to larger populations. For instance, the researcher could collect data from several schools across different regions to determine whether socioeconomic factors consistently correlate with academic performance (Figueiredo, Eloy, Marques, & Dias, 2023).

While this positivist method can yield statistically significant results and clear conclusions, it can also oversimplify complex social phenomena (Cohen et al., 2018). For instance, focusing solely on numerical data could overlook essential contexts, such as individual experiences or specific challenges faced by students from diverse backgrounds.

Post-Positivist Approach

In contrast, a post-positivist approach recognises the limitations of striving for complete objectivity and acknowledges the subjective nature of knowledge creation. Researchers adopting this perspective seek to explore the complexities of human experience and how various factors intertwine (Dawadi et al., 2021). For instance, in examining the same relationship between SES and educational attainment, a post-positivist researcher may employ:

Qualitative Methods: Qualitative methods, such as in-depth interviews with students and parents, provide rich insights into personal stories about educational journeys. Through this approach, researchers can explore how family expectations, cultural values, and available resources influence these experiences.

Conducting interviews allows participants to share their perspectives in detail, offering a deeper understanding of the factors that shape their educational paths. By analysing these narratives, researchers can identify themes and patterns that reveal the complexities of individual experiences within the educational system. This qualitative approach adds depth to the understanding of how various influences interact and impact students and their families. (Bazen et al., 2021).

Complex Interactions: Here, the researcher acknowledges that the relationship between SES and education is influenced by many factors, including individual agency (the capacity to make choices), social contexts (the environments in which individuals live), and historical circumstances. For example, understanding the impact of government policies on education funding could enrich the analysis (Pampel, Krueger, & Denney, 2010).

This approach aims not to establish universal laws but to develop nuanced, context-specific understandings of the phenomena being investigated. While post-positivist methods yield rich qualitative data that provide deep insights into social issues, they may challenge generalisability due to their focus on particular contexts (Tiokhin et al., 2019).

Interpretation of Findings - The differing approaches lead to significant variations in how findings are interpreted:

Positivist Research: This approach often seeks definitive conclusions, presenting results as objective truths supported by statistical evidence. For example, a positivist could focus on standardised test scores to establish clear policy recommendations in evaluating an educational intervention (De Vos et al., 2005).

Post-positivist Research: In contrast, post-positivist findings are seen as interpretations that are open to multiple perspectives. The researchers acknowledge the provisional nature of knowledge, emphasising the complexities of the social world (Dawadi et al., 2021). Continuing with our educational intervention example, a post-positivist could conduct qualitative interviews with students and teachers to assess the intervention's broader impact, potentially uncovering unintended consequences (Shannon-Baker, 2023).

Methodological Approaches

The choice of methodology directly reflects these philosophical stances:

Positivist Research: Typically favours controlled experimental designs to establish causal relationships through manipulating and testing of variables (De Vos et al., 2005).

Post-positivist Research: Often utilises naturalistic designs that embrace the complexities of the social world, acknowledging the challenge of fully controlling all factors (Horowitz, 2004).

A positivist may conduct a randomised controlled trial to evaluate a new therapy's effectiveness, ensuring strict control over variables for high internal validity.

Conversely, a post-positivist may employ a qualitative case study approach, exploring therapeutic experiences in a real-world context while recognising the intricate interplay of various factors (De Vos et al., 2005).

The ongoing evolution from strictly positivist approaches to incorporating post-positivist perspectives has broadened the scope of social science research. The limitations of relying solely on quantitative methods to address complex social phenomena have become evident, leading to an appreciation for qualitative methodologies and mixed-methods designs. As researchers critically reflect on their philosophical assumptions and methodological choices, this shift acknowledges the value of diverse approaches.

Integrating Approaches

The dialogue between positivism and post-positivism is not a strict dichotomy. Many researchers now integrate aspects of both paradigms:

Mixed-Methods Research: This increasingly popular approach combines quantitative and qualitative methods to understand social phenomena comprehensively. For instance, a study on the impact of social media on political polarisation could analyse social media data quantitatively while conducting qualitative interviews to understand how online interactions shape political views (Dawadi et al., 2021).

The choice between a positivist and post-positivist approach to research has significant implications for the entire research process. It shapes:

Research Questions: Determining the focus and nature of the inquiries posed.

Design and Methods: Influencing how researchers construct their studies and gather data.

Interpretation: Affecting how findings are understood and applied in real-world contexts.

While positivist approaches offer the advantage of generalisability and straightforward conclusions, they can sometimes oversimplify the complexities of social phenomena. In contrast, post-positivist approaches provide richer, nuanced understandings but may limit the applicability of findings to broader contexts. The ongoing dialogue between these paradigms continues to enhance the field of social science research, encouraging innovation while deepening our grasp of human behaviour and societal dynamics.

Ultimately, researchers should critically evaluate their philosophical assumptions and choose the most appropriate methodology for their specific research questions. Integrating mixed-methods research signifies a substantial advancement in the social sciences, allowing researchers to achieve a more comprehensive understanding of social phenomena than either approach could offer alone.

Hypothetical Case Study: Contrasting Positivist and Post-positivist Research Designs

To understand the practical differences between positivist and post-positivist research designs, let's consider a common research question: *What is the impact of social media use on adolescent self-esteem?* This inquiry is particularly relevant in today's digital age, where social media has become an integral part of young people's lives. However, how researchers approach this question can vary dramatically depending on their philosophical stance.

Positivist Approach: In a positivist framework, researchers begin with a clear and corresponding null hypotheses.

For instance, the positivist researcher could formulate their hypotheses as follows:

Null Hypothesis (H0): There is no relationship between social media use and adolescent self-esteem. **Alternative Hypothesis (H1):** Increased daily use of social media is associated with lower self-esteem in adolescents.

From here, the positivist researcher focuses on data collection and analysis to either accept or reject the null hypothesis.

1. Research Design:

The researcher designs a large-scale quantitative study, employing randomised controlled trials or surveys. They could survey hundreds of adolescents across different schools to gather data.

2. Data Collection:

Participants would be asked to report their social media usage (measured in hours spent on platforms) and their self-esteem levels (using established scales like the Rosenberg Self-Esteem Scale).

3. Data Analysis:

Statistical methods like regression analysis or correlation coefficients would be employed to examine relationships between social media usage and self-esteem. If the results indicate a statistically significant negative correlation, the null hypothesis would be rejected, supporting the alternative hypothesis. However, this approach yields clear results, yet it may overlook the complexity of individual experiences. For instance, a focus solely on numerical data may not take into account the differing effects social media has on self-esteem in various cultural and personal contexts.

Post-Positivist Approach: In contrast, a post-positivist researcher approaches the same question with a broader perspective, aiming to understand a range of experiences without rigid hypotheses. Instead of focusing strictly on causal relationships, they may ask: *Hypothetical Research Question: How do adolescents perceive their social media use concerning their self-esteem?*

This question opens the inquiry, allowing for exploring many factors without tying it to a specific null hypothesis.

1. Research Design:

The researcher could choose a mixed-methods design, integrating quantitative data collection with qualitative insights.

2. Data Collection:

Initially, they conducted a quantitative survey to gather data on social media usage and self-esteem, followed by qualitative interviews with a smaller group of adolescents to explore their feelings about social media and its impact on their self-esteem.

3. Data Analysis:

The data analysis involves both statistical evaluation of survey responses and thematic analysis of the interviews. This comprehensive approach allows for a deeper exploration of how social media influences self-esteem, revealing that for some adolescents, it provides support and connection, while for others, it leads to feelings of inadequacy.

Key Differences

Interpretation of Findings

The Clinical Trial Journey: Dr Blake and Dr Sarah

In a busy hospital, two researchers, Dr Blake and Dr Sarah, were conducting a clinical trial to test a new medication for treating adult anxiety. Both were dedicated to their work but approached the research from different philosophical perspectives.

Dr Blake's Positivist Approach

Dr Blake aimed to find clear and conclusive results through his trial. He believed that objective truths about the medication's effectiveness could be revealed by using rigorous methods. To achieve this, he set up a double-blind study, meaning that neither the participants nor the researchers knew who received the actual medication and who received a placebo.

Dr Blake recruited 200 participants diagnosed with anxiety disorders. After several weeks of treatment, he carefully analysed the data, focusing on measurable outcomes such as reduced anxiety scores from standardised tests.

When the results were in, Dr Blake found that the new medication significantly lowered anxiety levels compared to the placebo. He confidently presented his findings at a medical conference, stating, "This medication is effective for treating anxiety. These results are definitive and objective."

Dr Sarah's Post-Positivist Perspective

Meanwhile, Dr Sarah adopted a different approach. While she recognised the importance of quantifiable outcomes, she also understood the complexities of human emotions and behaviours. Her goal was to assess whether the medication worked and explore how participants experienced it.

Dr Sarah conducted the same clinical trial but added qualitative interviews with participants after the study. She posed questions such as, "How did you feel during the treatment?" and "What was your experience with the medication?"

As she reviewed her findings, Dr Sarah discovered that while many participants experienced reduced anxiety, some reported side effects that made the medication challenging to tolerate, impacting their overall experience. Additionally, some participants noted that the support they received during the trial played a crucial role in their improvement—an aspect not captured through purely quantitative measures.

Dr Sarah reflected, "The medication may have a statistically significant effect, but individual experiences vary widely based on context, support systems, and personal histories."

The Takeaway

After their trials, Dr Blake and Dr Sarah shared their findings with their colleagues. Dr Blake presented his clear, definitive results from the quantitative analysis, demonstrating the medication's effectiveness. In contrast, Dr Sarah contributed to the discussion by highlighting the nuanced experiences of the participants, revealing the medication's impact beyond mere numbers.

Their supervisor praised both approaches, stating, "Dr Blake's research gives us a strong understanding of the medication's efficacy, while Dr Sarah's findings remind us that patient experiences are significant. Each perspective enhances our overall understanding of treatment in the real world."

Through their exploration, Dr Blake and Dr Sarah recognised that while positivist research seeks clear, objective truths, post-positivist research embraces the complexity of human experience. Both perspectives are essential for developing effective treatments in the field of medicine.

In summary:

Positivist research typically aims for definitive conclusions and presents results as objective truths.

Post-positivist research acknowledges that findings are interpretations influenced by various contexts and emphasises the complexity of social phenomena.

<u>Methodological Focus</u>

Positivist studies typically rely on controlled experiments to establish causal relationships.

Post-positivist studies often employ naturalistic designs, recognising that social factors cannot always be controlled.

<u>Researcher's Role</u>

The positivist researcher seeks objectivity and minimises personal influence on the research process.

The post-positivist researcher acknowledges their subjective position, understanding that their values and beliefs shape the research question and interpretation of findings.

Table 5: Case Study: Contrasting Positivist and Post-positivist Research Designs

Aspect	Positivist Approach	Post-positivist Approach
Hypothesis	Formulated to test a specific relationship between variables.	More exploratory, seeking to understand varying influences and meanings.
Research Design	Large-scale quantitative study using a survey.	A mixed-methods approach combines quantitative surveys with qualitative interviews.
Data Collection	Standardised measures/scales.	In-depth interviews and focus groups to gather personal experiences.
Data Analysis	Statistical tests (correlation, regression) to determine the strength and direction of relationships.	Mixed analysis combining statistical trends and thematic analysis of qualitative data.
Goal	Identify statistically significant relationships that can be generalised to a larger population.	Develop nuanced, context-specific understandings of social phenomena based on lived experiences.
Interpretation of Findings	Objective truths, with a focus on statistical significance and causal links.	Findings are acknowledged as interpretations, emphasising context

Conclusion

This section highlights the significant differences between positivist and post-positivist research designs in studying the impact of social media on adolescent self-esteem. While positivism emphasises objectivity, generalisability, and testing hypotheses through quantitative methods, post-positivism embraces complexity and subjectivity, often utilising mixed-methods research.

The choice between these paradigms is not just a matter of preference; it reflects fundamental philosophical commitments shaping every aspect of the research process. Researchers should select the most appropriate approach based on their research questions, the phenomenon under investigation, and their philosophical stance. Ultimately, understanding these differences enhances the critical evaluation of research findings and contributes to the ongoing evolution of social science methodology. The growing integration of mixed-methods approaches reflects a trend toward more comprehensive insights into complex social issues, fostering a richer dialogue between positivist and post-positivist perspectives in the future of social science research.

CHAPTER 2: POSITIVIST RESEARCH DESIGNS

EXPERIMENTAL DESIGNS IN POSITIVIST RESEARCH

Experimental designs are fundamental to positivist research, focusing on establishing cause-and-effect relationships through controlled manipulation of variables. A key feature of true experiments is the random assignment of participants to different conditions, which helps ensure comparability and minimises the influence of confounding variables (extraneous factors that could affect the outcome) (S. Mishra & Datta-Gupta, 2018).

1. Key Features of Experimental Designs

Internal Validity: One of the key features of experimental designs is internal validity, which is primarily achieved through random assignment of participants to different groups. This process ensures that any observed effects can be confidently attributed to the independent variable being tested, rather than to other confounding factors. By controlling for variables and ensuring that groups are equivalent at the start of the experiment, researchers can make stronger claims about causation and the relationship between variables. This emphasis on internal validity is essential for establishing the credibility of the experimental findings. (Patino & Ferreira, 2018).

Randomised Controlled Trials (RCTs): Considered the gold standard in experimental design RCTs involve the random assignment of participants to either a control group or an experimental group, which helps eliminate bias and ensures that any differences observed can be attributed to the treatment or intervention being tested.

Since it enhances the reliability of the findings, RCTs are a critical tool in fields such as healthcare, psychology, and social sciences for evaluating the effectiveness of interventions. (Hariton & Locascio, 2018). In a RCT designed to evaluate educational methods, researchers might compare a new teaching method against a traditional method. Typically, participants would be randomly assigned to either the experimental group, which employs the new teaching approach, or the control group, which continues with the traditional method. The effectiveness of each teaching method would be measured based on specific performance metrics, such as test scores, engagement levels, or retention of information. By analysing the outcomes, researchers can determine whether the new method leads to significantly improved performance compared to the traditional approaches (Sovacool et al., 2018).

While RCTs provide robust evidence due to careful variable control, they may not always be feasible or ethical, especially in social science research. In such cases, **quasi-experimental designs** become a viable alternative, although they lack the complete control of true experiments (Schweizer, Braun, & Milstone, 2016).

2. Quasi-Experimental Designs

Comparison Groups: Quasi-experimental designs involve using comparison groups to evaluate the effects of an intervention when random assignment is not feasible. In this approach, researchers create or identify similar groups but do not randomly assign participants to these groups. By comparing an experimental group that receives the intervention to a control or comparison group that does not, researchers can assess the impact of the intervention on outcomes. While quasi-experimental designs are less rigorous than true experimental designs due to the lack of randomisation, they still provide valuable insights, particularly in real-world settings where ethical or practical constraints may limit random assignment. Researchers should carefully consider potential confounding variables and employ statistical methods to account for group differences. (Rutkowski, Rutkowski, Thompson, & Canbolat, 2024).

Matching Techniques: In quasi-experimental designs, matching techniques are employed to enhance the comparability of participants in different groups. This involves pairing individuals from the experimental and comparison groups based on similar characteristics, such as age, gender, socio-economic status, or baseline performance levels (McCambridge, Witton, & Elbourne, 2014).

By ensuring that these matched participants share key traits, researchers can reduce the impact of confounding variables that may influence the outcomes. This process aims to create more equivalent groups, thereby enhancing the validity of the comparisons between the intervention's effects and the control condition. Although matching does not eliminate all biases associated with lack of random assignment, it strengthens the design by improving the overall comparability of the groups involved. (McCambridge et al., 2014).

Interrupted Time Series Design: This quasi-experimental method involves measuring the dependent variable multiple times before and after an intervention. This approach allows researchers to observe the effects of the intervention over time, providing a clearer picture of trends and changes in the variable of interest (Handley, Lyles, McCulloch, & Cattamanchi, 2018).

By collecting data at several points, researchers can identify patterns and fluctuations in the dependent variable that occur as a result of the intervention. This design helps to control for potential threats to validity that may arise from external factors, as it assesses how the variable behaves in response to the intervention over a defined period. Interrupted time series designs are particularly useful for evaluating the impact of policies, programmes, or changes in practice within real-world settings. (Handley et al., 2018).

Researchers decide between experimental and quasi-experimental designs based on several factors, including their research question, available resources, and ethical considerations. Experimental designs are typically preferred if the focus is on establishing cause-and-effect relationships. However, quasi-experimental designs may be more suitable if the aim is to understand real-world situations (Sovacool et al., 2018). Experimental designs often require more time, participants, and funding due to the need for strict control and random assignment. In contrast, quasi-experimental designs can be more practical when resources are limited. Additionally, randomly assigning participants to different conditions may not always be ethical, especially in sensitive studies. Quasi-experimental designs allow researchers to investigate these situations without random assignment (S. Mishra & Datta-Gupta, 2018).

Ultimately, the goal is to maximise internal validity, ensuring that the results accurately demonstrate cause-and-effect relationships while also considering external validity, which allows the findings to be generalised to other contexts.

Causal Inferences and Limitations

While well-designed experiments provide strong evidence for causal inferences, it is crucial to acknowledge their limitations. No study can definitively prove causality; experimental designs yield compelling support for causal claims by controlling alternative explanations and reducing confounding variables (Rutkowski et al., 2024).

3. Enhancements to Experimental Designs

Factorial Designs: Factorial designs are enhancements to experimental designs that allow researchers to investigate the effects of multiple independent variables and their interactions simultaneously. This approach provides a more comprehensive understanding of complex phenomena by examining how various factors influence outcomes together rather than in isolation.(Watkins & Newbold, 2020). For example, a study could explore both teaching methods and class size on student achievement. By using a factorial design, researchers could create different combinations of teaching methods (e.g., traditional vs. innovative) and class sizes (e.g., small vs. large) to determine not only the main effects of each variable but also how they interact with one another. This nuanced perspective allows for deeper insights into how multiple factors work together to impact student performance, informing more effective educational practices and policies.

Blinding Techniques:
Blinding techniques are critical enhancements in experimental designs aimed at reducing bias.

Single-Blind Studies: In single-blind studies, participants are unaware of their assigned group, which helps to mitigate placebo effects—improvements that occur due to participants' expectations rather than the actual treatment (Watkins & Newbold, 2020).

By keeping participants blind to whether they are in the experimental or control group, researchers can obtain more accurate data on the effects of the intervention. This technique ensures that any observed changes can be more confidently attributed to the treatment rather than participants' expectations or beliefs about the intervention. Single-blind designs are particularly useful in studies where expectations might influence participant behaviour and outcomes.

Double-Blind Studies: Double-blind studies are an advanced blinding technique in experimental designs where both participants and researchers are unaware of group assignments. This approach minimises bias from both sides, as it prevents participants' expectations and researchers' influences from affecting the outcomes. (Monaghan et al., 2021).By keeping both groups blind to the treatment conditions, double-blind studies enhance the integrity of the research. Participants do not know whether they are receiving the intervention or a placebo, reducing the likelihood of placebo effects. Simultaneously, researchers cannot unintentionally influence participants' responses or data collection, helping to maintain objectivity in the results. This method is particularly valuable in clinical trials and other settings where bias can significantly impact the interpretation of the effectiveness of an intervention (Monaghan et al., 2021).

Example One: *Randomised Controlled Trials and Quasi-experimental Design*

At a respected university, researchers Dr Emma and Dr James decided to conduct a study to determine the most effective teaching methods. Their exploration into experimental designs would reveal important insights about the research process.

Dr Emma's Use of Experimental Designs

Dr Emma focused on positivist research methods, believing that establishing clear cause-and-effect relationships was fundamental. She designed a true experiment where she could control the variables in her study. "To determine which teaching method is most effective," she stated, "we need to manipulate teaching approaches and observe their effects on student performance."

Dr Emma recruited a diverse group of 100 students and randomly assigned them to two conditions: one group learned using an innovative teaching method, while the other followed a traditional approach. This random assignment was critical; it ensured that each group was comparable and minimised the influence of extraneous factors.

Key Features of Experimental Designs

Dr Emma recognised that a key feature of experimental designs is internal validity. By randomly assigning participants, she could assert that any differences in student performance were due to the teaching method rather than other influences. This was essential for drawing reliable conclusions.

The Gold Standard: Randomised Controlled Trials

To illustrate the strength of her method, Dr Emma explained to her colleagues the concept of Randomised Controlled Trials (RCTs). "RCTs are the gold standard in experimental design," she noted. "When comparing a new teaching method against a traditional one, we can measure effectiveness based on student performance."

Dr Emma collected data on the students' scores as the study progressed. The results indicated that the innovative method significantly improved performance, confirming her hypothesis. Her carefully controlled study provided evidence regarding the effectiveness of the new approach.

Dr James's Perspective on Real-World Challenges Using a Quasi-experimental Design

Conversely, Dr James was interested in the complexities of real-world applications. He acknowledged the rigour of RCTs but also recognised that such methods may not always be feasible or ethical in specific contexts. "It is not always possible to manipulate variables as Dr Emma did," he remarked. "In practical situations, challenges can arise."

For instance, if Dr James aimed to study the impact of a new reading programme in schools, he may not be able to randomly assign some schools to use it and others not, as this could affect students' learning experiences and wellbeing. Instead, he opted for a quasi-experimental design, comparing schools already using the programme with those that were not. While this approach lacked the complete control of true experiments, it still allowed him to gather relevant insights.

The Takeaway

In their discussions, Dr Emma and Dr James shared their findings with their peers. Dr Emma's experiment demonstrated how experimental designs effectively establish cause-and-effect relationships, offering precise answers to educational questions. In contrast, Dr James highlighted the significance of considering ethical implications and real-world contexts when designing research.

Their supervisor acknowledged both approaches, stating, "While Dr Emma's RCT provided evidence of effectiveness, Dr James's quasi-experiment illustrates that research should also adapt to the complexities of real-world situations."

Example Two: *Experimental Enhancements using a Factorial Design*

At Elmwood University, a research team led by Dr Helen set out to explore strategies for enhancing student achievement in mathematics. Aiming to design a robust study, they incorporated several enhancements to their experimental design to gain clearer insights into effective teaching methods.

Exploring Multiple Factors: **A Factorial Design**

Dr Helen recognised that understanding the impact of both teaching methods and class sizes on student achievement was essential. Rather than studying each factor in isolation, she implemented a factorial design, which allowed her to investigate multiple independent variables and their interactions.

She organised her study into four groups: one group experienced traditional teaching methods in a small class setting, another engaged with innovative, technology-based learning in a small class, a third received traditional teaching in a larger class, and the final group combined technology-based learning with a larger class size.

By using this factorial design, Dr Helen and her team aimed to uncover how combining teaching methods and class sizes influenced student performance.

After several months of data collection, they discovered notable insights: students in small classes using technology-based methods outperformed their peers, while those in larger classes struggled, regardless of the teaching style. This nuanced view provided a comprehensive understanding of the factors contributing to student success.

Incorporating Blinding Techniques for Validity

To enhance the validity of her study, Dr Helen also implemented blinding techniques to minimise potential bias. She recognised that expectations could influence outcomes, so she designed a single-blind study, meaning participants were unaware of which teaching method they were receiving. This approach helped reduce the placebo effect, where students may feel they performed better simply because they knew they were part of a study. Dr Helen aimed to obtain more authentic results by keeping participants unaware of their assigned group.

For added rigour, her study was structured as a double-blind experiment in a later phase, ensuring that not only were the participants unaware of their group assignments, but the researchers administering the teaching methods also did not know which approach each group was receiving. This ensured that personal biases from the researchers did not influence student behaviour or data collection.

The Results and Insights

Upon concluding the study, Dr Helen and her team analysed the data, revealing clear patterns. Combining small class sizes and innovative teaching methods significantly improved student achievement. Moreover, implementing both blinding techniques led to more reliable results, minimising the influence of expectations and biases.

Dr Helen presented her findings at a national education conference, emphasising the importance of factorial designs for considering multiple variables and the necessity of blinding techniques to enhance the validity of educational research. She shared how these enhancements provided richer insights into tailoring teaching methods for optimal student performance.

4. Data Analysis

Statistical tests (e.g., t-tests, ANOVA) evaluate the significance of observed effects, determining whether differences between groups likely result from the independent variable rather than chance. Effect sizes (quantification of the magnitude of effects) provide additional context, helping researchers interpret findings beyond statistical significance.

Interpretation of Findings

Interpreting experimental findings requires careful consideration of factors such as:

Generalisability: Interpreting findings from ANOVA (Analysis of Variance) requires careful consideration of several factors, including generalisability. Generalisability refers to the extent to which the study results can be applied to a broader population beyond the sample used in the research (Hariton & Locascio, 2018). The degree of generalisability largely depends on the sample's representativeness and the similarity of the context in which the study was conducted to other settings. If the sample includes a diverse range of participants that accurately reflects the target population and the study conditions are comparable to real-world scenarios, the findings can be more confidently generalised.

Limitations: Transparency about sample size, biases, and specific participant characteristics allows for informed evaluation of the study's conclusions. If the sample is limited in diversity or the context is unique, the ability to extrapolate the results to other groups or situations may be compromised. Therefore, researchers should critically assess these factors when interpreting ANOVA findings to ensure valid conclusions.

Example Three: *Using T-Tests and ANOVA*

At Crestwood College, Dr Oliver initiated a research project to evaluate the effectiveness of a new reading intervention program for struggling students. After extensive data collection, he analysed the results to extract meaningful insights.

<u>Diving into Data Analysis</u>

With a substantial dataset, Dr Oliver began the critical data analysis phase. He employed various statistical tests, including t-tests and ANOVA (Analysis of Variance), to evaluate the significance of the observed effects.

The t-test was useful for comparing the means of two groups: the intervention group (participants in the new programme) and the control group (those receiving standard instruction). Dr Oliver calculated the t-test to determine whether the difference in average reading scores between the two groups was statistically significant, suggesting that it was unlikely to have occurred by chance. He examined the p-value produced by the test; if it fell below a predetermined threshold (commonly set at 0.05), he could conclude that the new reading programme had a meaningful impact on student performance.

For more comprehensive analysis, Dr Oliver utilised ANOVA. This method allowed him to investigate whether different teaching methodologies within the programme also significantly affected reading achievement. ANOVA enabled him to compare the means of three or more groups simultaneously, allowing for a deeper understanding of how multiple variables may interact. By assessing the variation between the groups in relation to the variation within the groups, ANOVA assisted him in determining if at least one group exhibited a statistically significant difference from the others.

Upon completing these analyses, Dr Oliver identified a significant difference in reading scores, indicating that the new programme positively affected student outcomes. He also calculated effect sizes to quantify the magnitude of the differences observed, providing further context for interpreting his findings. For instance, he noted that the new programme improved reading scores and contributed to a notable increase in students' confidence.

Careful Interpretation of Findings

After concluding the data analysis, Dr Oliver focused on interpreting the findings. He recognised that meaningful conclusions required careful consideration of several factors.

First, he evaluated the generalisability of his results. Dr Oliver understood that the extent to which his findings could be applied to a broader population depended on the representativeness of his sample and the context similarities. Although he had collected data from a diverse group of students at Crestwood College, he questioned whether the results would apply to other schools with varying demographics.

Next, he addressed the study's limitations. Dr Oliver was transparent about the sample size and acknowledged that, while reasonably large, certain participant characteristics—such as varying levels of motivation and home support—could influence the results. By discussing these limitations, he enabled others to assess the conclusions drawn from his study critically.

Presenting the Findings

When Dr Oliver presented his findings at the annual education conference, he shared both the statistical results and their implications for educational practice. He noted that the new reading intervention programme led to improved academic outcomes as well as an increase in students' confidence in their reading abilities.His analysis and interpretation provided valuable insights for educators and researchers, highlighting the importance of considering both statistical significance and practical implications in their own studies. Through this research journey, Dr Oliver demonstrated how effective data analysis and careful interpretation of findings can enhance our understanding of educational interventions. His work added to the existing body of knowledge in the field, offering a basis for further exploration and application of effective teaching practices.

Conclusion

Experimental designs are powerful tools in positivist research for exploring cause-and-effect relationships. Both randomised controlled trials and quasi-experimental designs, combined with appropriate statistical analysis, provide strong evidence for causal inferences. However, researchers should be mindful of limitations and aim to maximise both internal and external validity through thoughtful planning and rigorous execution. Transparency in reporting study designs, limitations, and findings is vital for maintaining research integrity and credibility. This critical assessment of biases and confounding variables fosters a more accurate interpretation of results, contributing to a deeper understanding of social phenomena. The ongoing development of experimental techniques and statistical analysis continues to enhance the effectiveness of this essential research approach.

Table 6: Breaking down Positivist Research Designs

Aspect	Details
Definition	Experimental designs focus on establishing cause-and-effect relationships through controlled manipulation of variables.
Key Features of Experimental Designs	- **Internal Validity**: Confirming that the independent variable causes observed effects. - **Randomised Controlled Trials (RCTs)**: comparing a new teaching method with a traditional one.
Quasi-Experimental Designs	- **Comparison Groups**: Used to compare groups without random assignment. - **Matching Techniques**: Participants are paired based on similar characteristics to improve comparability. - **Interrupted Time Series Design**: Measures the dependent variable multiple times before and after an intervention to observe effects.
Example of Quasi-Experimental Design	Studying crime rates before and after a new policing strategy to identify changes associated with the intervention.
Research Design Goals	Aim to maximise internal validity while considering external validity (generalisability).
Causal Inferences and Limitations	Experimental designs provide strong evidence for causal claims but can never definitively prove causation.
Enhancements to Experimental Designs	- **Factorial Designs**: Investigate multiple independent variables and their interactions. - **Blinding Techniques**: - **Single-Blind Studies**: Participants were unaware of their group assignment. - **Double-Blind Studies**: Both participants and researchers are unaware of group assignments.
Data Analysis	Involves statistical tests (e.g., t-tests, ANOVA) to evaluate the significance of observed effects.
Interpretation of Findings	- **Generalisability**: Depends on sample representativeness and context similarity. - **Limitations**: Transparency in sample size, biases, and characteristics enhances the evaluation of the study conclusions.

NON-EXPERIMENTAL DESIGNS WITHIN THE POSITIVIST FRAMEWORK

While experimental designs are central to positivist research, researchers should be mindful to ensure feasibility and that they are ethical. Non-experimental designs offer valuable insights by relying on observation and measurement of variables without manipulation, seeking to identify relationships and patterns (Lobmeier, 2010).

1. Correlational Studies

Correlational studies investigate relationships between two or more variables without manipulating any variables. This approach allows researchers to examine how changes in one variable are associated with changes in another, identifying patterns or trends (Edmonds & Kennedy, 2017).

Instead of determining cause-and-effect relationships, correlational studies focus on the strength and direction of associations. For example, a study could explore the correlation between study time and academic performance, revealing whether increased study time is associated with higher grades.

While these studies provide valuable insights into relationships, it is essential to note that correlation does not imply causation; other factors may influence the observed associations. Therefore, correlational studies are useful for generating hypotheses and guiding further research but should be interpreted cautiously regarding causative conclusions (Akoglu, 2018). Key points include:

Measurement of Relationships: In correlational studies, relationships are measured using correlation coefficients, which quantify both the strength and direction of the relationship between variables. These coefficients range from -1 to +1 (Edmonds & Kennedy, 2017). A coefficient of -1 indicates a perfect negative correlation, meaning that as one variable increases, the other decreases in a perfectly predictable manner. A coefficient of +1 signifies a perfect positive correlation, indicating that as one variable increases, the other also increases correspondingly. A value of 0 reflects no correlation, suggesting that there is no discernible relationship between the variables (De Vos et al., 2005).

By calculating and interpreting these correlation coefficients, researchers can gauge the degree to which variables are related, guiding further investigation into potential causal relationships. (De Vos et al., 2005).

Caution: Caution is essential when interpreting correlational studies, as correlation does not imply causation. For example, a positive correlation between the number of firefighters at a scene and the amount of damage caused by a fire does not mean that more firefighters cause greater damage. Instead, larger fires require more firefighters, which means both variables are linked to the severity of the fire rather than one causing the other.

This example highlights the importance of careful interpretation of correlational data. Researchers must consider other potential variables and external factors that could influence the observed relationships, underscoring the need for further research to establish causality.

Researchers use advanced statistical methods to control for confounding variables. Techniques like multiple regression analysis help assess the independent effects of various predictors on an outcome variable.

2. Surveys

Surveys are widely used in positivist research to systematically collect data from individuals. This method allows researchers to gather quantifiable information on various topics, such as attitudes, opinions, behaviours, and demographic characteristics (Shiyanbola et al., 2021).

Surveys typically employ structured questionnaires with closed-ended questions that facilitate statistical analysis of the responses. By ensuring that the sample is representative of the larger population, researchers can generalise their findings and draw meaningful conclusions. The systematic approach of surveys helps to minimise bias and improve the reliability of the data collected, making them a valuable tool for positivist research aimed at understanding trends and patterns within populations. (Sapsford, 2007):

Data Collection: Data collection in surveys involves gathering large amounts of information on attitudes, beliefs, behaviours, and demographic characteristics through structured questionnaires or interviews (Shiyanbola et al., 2021).

Questionnaires typically consist of predetermined questions that participants respond to, allowing for efficient data collection and subsequent statistical analysis. Alternatively, interviews may be conducted to obtain more in-depth responses, although they tend to be less structured than questionnaires.

By employing these methods, surveys can compile a comprehensive dataset that reflects the perspectives and experiences of a broad population, enabling researchers to identify trends and relationships among the variables studied. This systematic data gathering is crucial for informing conclusions and developing insights in positivist research (De Vos et al., 2005).

Generalisation: This refers to the ability to apply findings from a study to a broader population, and this capability largely depends on the representativeness of the sample used. Researchers employ various sampling techniques to enhance generalisability, including (Hariton & Locascio, 2018):

Random Sampling: This method ensures that every individual in the population has an equal chance of being selected for the study. This approach reduces bias and increases the likelihood that the sample accurately reflects the larger population (Sibbald & Roland, 1998).

Stratified Sampling: In this technique, the population is divided into subgroups, or strata, based on specific characteristics (e.g., age, gender, socioeconomic status). Researchers then sample from each subgroup, ensuring representation across key dimensions and improving the overall representativeness of the sample (De Vos et al., 2005).

Cluster Sampling: Instead of sampling individuals directly, this method randomly selects groups or clusters (e.g., schools, neighbourhoods) and then samples individuals within those clusters. This approach can be more practical and cost-effective, particularly when dealing with large populations (De Vos et al., 2005).

The quality of survey instruments is crucial, as poorly designed questions can lead to misleading results. Ambiguous, leading, or confusing questions may distort respondents' answers, ultimately compromising the validity of the data collected (Heale & Twycross, 2015).

To mitigate these risks, pretesting questions is an essential step in the survey development process. Pretesting involves administering the survey to a small group of individuals representative of the target population to identify potential issues such as unclear wording, question bias, or response format problems (Heale & Twycross, 2015).

Gathering feedback during this phase allows researchers to refine and improve the survey instrument, ensuring that questions accurately capture the intended information. This careful attention to question design enhances the reliability and validity of the survey results, contributing to more meaningful and actionable insights. (De Vos et al., 2005).

3. Observational Studies

Observational studies within the positivist framework involve systematically observing and recording behaviour in natural settings without manipulating variables. This structured approach emphasises predefined categories and criteria for behaviours, minimising subjectivity and bias, thus ensuring that the data collected can be quantified and statistically analysed (De Vos et al., 2005).

By focusing on structured observations, researchers can maintain high ecological validity, capturing how individuals behave in real-world contexts. This method allows for the identification of patterns and trends that may not be visible through experimental designs. However, researchers must be cautious about bias in their observations, as personal interpretations can still influence the recorded data (Cohen et al., 2018).

Types of Observation

In positivism, different types of observation are employed to systematically study behaviour in natural settings.

These include:

Naturalistic Observation: This method involves observing behaviour as it occurs naturally, with minimal interference from the researcher. This approach allows for the collection of data in real-world contexts, maintaining ecological validity (Busetto et al., 2020).

Structured Observation: This type of observation uses predefined categories to guide data collection, ensuring consistency across observations. By standardising the data collection process, researchers can enhance reliability and facilitate quantitative analysis (De Vos et al., 2005).

Participant Observation: While traditional participant observation involves the researcher actively engaging in the environment, quantitative researchers often adopt structured observation methods to collect data. In this approach, researchers maintain a passive observer role, focusing on gathering quantifiable data while minimising their influence on participants' actions.

Non-Participant Observation In this method, the researcher remains detached from the setting, which helps reduce bias in the data collected. However, this detachment may result in missing some contextual depth that could provide valuable insights into the observed behaviours.

An example of non-participant observation on a broader scale could be a study conducted to examine pedestrian behaviour in a busy urban area, such as a city square or a transit station. In this case, researchers may set up multiple video cameras at various locations throughout the area to record the movements and interactions of thousands of pedestrians over a significant period. By remaining detached from the setting, the researchers can gather large amounts of data on aspects such as traffic patterns, social interactions, and group dynamics without influencing how individuals behave.

4. Archival Research

Archival research utilises existing data such as historical documents, census records, or media archives (Gaillet, 2012):

Valuable for Historical Trends: This approach is invaluable for understanding societal changes over time, as it allows researchers to access a wealth of data, including government records, letters, photographs, and organisational documents.

By analysing these materials, researchers can gain insights into the cultural, economic, and political contexts of different periods. Archival research helps to construct narratives around historical events, revealing how societies have evolved and responded to various challenges. It enables an exploration of long-term trends, providing a foundation for understanding contemporary issues in light of their historical roots. Overall, archival research is essential for enriching our comprehension of past dynamics and their influence on present and future developments.

Data Quality: In archival research, evaluating data quality is essential for ensuring valid findings. Researchers must assess the reliability and limitations of archival data, which may not include all necessary variables. The quality of records can vary due to factors like data collection methods and potential biases of the authors. Additionally, some relevant information may be missing or incomplete.

To address these issues, researchers should critically assess the data's provenance and consider supplementary sources when needed. By understanding these limitations, they can enhance the robustness of their analyses.

5. Case Studies

Case studies offer deeper analyses of a particular individual, group, event, or phenomenon:

Depth Over Breadth: Quantitative research focuses on measuring and analysing numerical data to uncover patterns and test hypotheses. It typically prioritises breadth over depth, allowing researchers to gather extensive data sets that can be generalised across larger populations (Edmonds & Kennedy, 2017).

However, in certain contexts, depth can take precedence. For example, case studies within a positivist framework collect quantitative data to investigate specific phenomena in detail. These studies can yield valuable insights into complex interactions, despite their limitations in generalisation. By providing a robust framework for hypothesis testing and theory development, quantitative research emphasises objectivity and employs rigorous methods. This balance ensures that researchers can draw meaningful conclusions while acknowledging the intricate nature of the subjects they study (Patino & Ferreira, 2018).

Multiple Case Studies: Multiple case studies involve the comparative analysis of different cases to enhance the trustworthiness and generalisability of research findings. By examining various instances of a phenomenon, researchers can identify patterns and contrasts that provide deeper insights. This approach employs triangulation, which involves using various methods and data sources to corroborate results .

Triangulation strengthens the validity of the findings by cross-verifying data, reducing biases associated with a single case study.

As a result, multiple case studies can yield more robust conclusions, allowing researchers to draw broader inferences and enhance the applicability of their results across different contexts. By integrating diverse perspectives and methods, this approach enriches the understanding of complex issues and contributes to more reliable and actionable insights (Patton, 1999).

A Fictional Exploration of Student Wellbeing: A Case Study at Oakwood School

At Oakwood School, which hosts a diverse community of learners, Dr Rachel, an educational researcher, aimed to understand the factors influencing student wellbeing. She employed various research methods to gather comprehensive data to achieve this goal.

Correlational Studies: Uncovering Relationships

To begin her research, Dr Rachel conducted a correlational study to explore the relationships among various factors, such as students' physical activity levels, academic performance, and overall wellbeing. She gathered data on multiple variables and calculated correlation coefficients, which indicate the strength and direction of relationships between them. A coefficient close to +1 suggests a strong positive correlation, while one near -1 indicates a strong negative correlation. A value of 0 signifies no correlation.

Dr Rachel emphasised caution in interpreting her findings. For example, if her study revealed a positive correlation between ice cream sales and crime rates, she noted that this did not imply that ice cream caused crime; rather, both may be influenced by summer heat. She controlled for confounding variables using advanced statistical methods, such as multiple regression analysis, to assess the independent effects of various predictors on student wellbeing.

Surveys: Gathering Large-Scale Data

Next, Dr Rachel designed a survey to collect extensive data on students' attitudes, beliefs, behaviours, and demographics. By distributing questionnaires to a diverse sample of students, she aimed to gather a large amount of information systematically.

She implemented rigorous sampling techniques to ensure her findings would be generalisable to the wider student population. Random sampling was utilised to give every student an equal chance of selection, while stratified sampling ensured representation across different year groups. Additionally, she employed cluster sampling by randomly selecting classes and administering the survey within those groups.

Understanding that the quality of survey instruments is crucial, Dr Rachel pretested her questions to identify potential issues and ensure clarity. This step helped her collect reliable data, avoiding misleading conclusions.

Observational Studies: Insights from Behaviour

Dr Rachel recognised that direct observation can yield valuable insights. She conducted structured observational studies focusing on quantifiable behaviours within natural settings. This approach allowed her to maintain a passive observer role, minimising her influence on the student's actions while collecting measurable data.

Using structured observation methods, she developed predefined categories for recording student interactions, ensuring consistency in data collection across various contexts. This enabled her to gather reliable quantitative data on student behaviours during classroom activities and recess without impacting the observed behaviours.

Archival Research: Examining Historical Trends

To enhance her research further, Dr Rachel turned to archival research, analysing existing data from historical documents, census records, and school archives. This method provided insights into societal changes and the evolving nature of student wellbeing.

While this approach was beneficial, Dr Rachel critically evaluated the quality of the archival data, recognising that it may not include all the necessary variables to support her hypotheses.

Positivist Case Studies: Analyses of Unique Experiences

Dr Rachel utilised case studies to conduct focused analyses of students with unique experiences affecting their wellbeing. In these case studies, she combined quantitative data collection methods, including structured observations, surveys with closed-ended questions, and analysis of existing numerical data from documents and archives. Sometimes, experiments were also conducted, targeting the specific circumstances of each case.

Evaluating multiple cases from case files allowed Dr Rachel to compare various individuals, identifying common themes while focusing on deeper understanding. This triangulation of methods and data sources strengthened the validity of her findings regarding student wellbeing.

Summary and Contributions

After her research, Dr Rachel compiled her findings and presented them to the Oakwood School board. She illustrated how various factors influenced student wellbeing, combining quantitative data from surveys and correlational studies with qualitative insights from observational studies and case analyses.

Her rigorous methodology and diverse approaches contributed to a deeper understanding of student wellbeing and laid the groundwork for future initiatives to enhance the overall school environment.

Conclusion

Experimental designs provide strong evidence for causal relationships within the positivist framework. However, non-experimental designs—such as correlational studies, surveys, observational studies, archival research, and case studies—also offer essential insights. Each design has strengths and weaknesses, so researchers should carefully consider these aspects when choosing their methods.

The effective application of statistical techniques, thorough data collection, and careful interpretation of findings are vital for maintaining scientific rigour and validity in non-experimental research. Researchers can comprehensively understand complex social issues by integrating various designs and approaches, reinforcing the importance of diverse research strategies within the positivist framework.

QUANTITATIVE DATA ANALYSIS TECHNIQUES

Having established the range of non-experimental designs within the positivist paradigm, we now turn to the role of quantitative data analysis techniques in drawing meaningful conclusions from collected data. The choice of statistical method is closely linked to the research question, the type of data, and the specific research design. This section will highlight key techniques used in positivist research alongside their applications, assumptions, and limitations (De Vos et al., 2005).

1. Regression Analysis

Regression analysis examines the relationship between a dependent variable (the outcome) and one or more independent variables (predictors) (John', Labrador, Younas, & Ali, 2021).

Linear Regression: Assumes a straight-line relationship between variables. It estimates the strength and direction of this relationship using regression coefficients (numbers that represent the degree of association). A positive coefficient indicates a positive association, while a negative coefficient suggests the opposite (Gordon, 2015).

Assumptions: Includes linearity (the relationship is a straight line), independence of errors (the residuals, or differences between actual and predicted values, are uncorrelated), and homoscedasticity (constant variance of errors). Violations of these assumptions can lead to inaccurate estimates.

2. t-Tests

The t-test compares the means (averages) of two groups to assess if there is a significant difference.

Independent Samples t-Test: An Independent Samples t-Test is a statistical method used to compare the means of two different groups to determine if there is a significant difference between them. This test is appropriate when the two groups are independent of one another, meaning that the individuals in one group do not overlap with those in the other (Kim, 2014a).

For example, a researcher may use an independent samples t-test to compare the average test scores of male and female students in a particular class. By calculating the t-statistic, the researcher can assess whether any observed difference in test scores between the two groups is statistically significant or may have occurred by chance. This test helps to determine if gender impacts academic performance within the studied context.

Paired Samples t-Test: A Paired Samples t-Test is a statistical method used to compare the means of the same group measured at two different times or under two different conditions. This test is appropriate when the measurements are dependent or related, allowing researchers to assess changes over time or the effects of an intervention (P. Mishra, Singh, Pandey, Mishra, & Pandey, 2019). For example, a researcher may conduct a study to evaluate the effectiveness of a training programme on student performance. The students' test scores could be measured before the training (pre-test scores) and again after the training (post-test scores). The paired samples t-test would allow the researcher to determine if there is a statistically significant difference between the pre-test and post-test scores, indicating whether the training programme positively impacted student performance.

Interpretation: Interpreting the results from statistical tests, such as the independent samples t-test or paired samples t-test, involves examining the p-value derived from the analysis. The p-value indicates the probability that any observed difference between groups (or measurements) is due to chance rather than a true effect.

For example, suppose a researcher conducts an independent samples t-test to compare the average test scores of two groups of students: Group A (who received a new teaching method) and Group B (who followed the traditional method). After performing the test, the researcher finds a p-value of 0.03. This p-value is below the standard threshold of 0.05, suggesting that the difference in average test scores between the two groups is statistically significant. This means there is only a 3% probability that the observed difference is due to random chance, implying that the new teaching method likely impacted student performance.

In another example, a researcher uses a paired samples t-test to evaluate the effectiveness of a wellness program by measuring participants' stress levels before and after the program. After analysis, the researcher obtains a p-value of 0.08. Since this p-value is above 0.05, it suggests that the difference in stress levels before and after the program is not statistically significant. In this case, the researcher would conclude that any observed change in stress levels could likely be attributed to chance rather than the wellness program itself. These examples illustrate how p-values help researchers determine whether their findings are statistically significant, guiding them in interpreting the results of their analyses.

3. Analysis of Variance (ANOVA)

ANOVA (Analysis of Variance) extends the capabilities of the t-test by allowing researchers to compare means across three or more groups. Unlike the t-test, which is limited to two groups, ANOVA is designed to evaluate whether there are any statistically significant differences among the means of multiple groups simultaneously. (Kim, 2014b). For example, suppose a researcher is interested in studying the effects of different teaching methods on student performance. They might have three groups of students: one group taught using a traditional method, another group using an online method, and a third group using an interactive method. By applying ANOVA, the researcher can determine if there are significant differences in average test scores among these three groups.

If the ANOVA results yield a p-value below the threshold of 0.05, the researcher would conclude that at least one group differs significantly in its mean test scores compared to the others. However, ANOVA does not specify which groups are different; further post-hoc tests would be needed to identify the specific group differences.

<u>Types of ANOVA</u>

One-Way ANOVA: One-Way ANOVA is a statistical method that compares means across one independent variable with multiple levels or categories.

This approach is particularly useful when researchers want to assess the impact of a single factor on a dependent variable.(Kim, 2014b). For example, a researcher investigating the effectiveness of different teaching methods on student performance might set up a study with three groups of students, each using a different teaching method: traditional, online, and interactive. Here, the independent variable is the teaching method, which has three levels.

By applying a One-Way ANOVA, the researcher can determine if there are significant differences in the average test scores among the three groups. If the ANOVA results indicate a p-value below 0.05, the researcher would conclude that at least one teaching method results in a different mean score compared to the others.

However, like other ANOVA designs, One-Way ANOVA does not specify which specific groups differ from each other. The researcher would need to conduct post-hoc tests after finding significant results to identify the exact differences among the groups. This method allows for a clear and efficient way to compare means when dealing with multiple levels of a single independent variable.

Two-way ANOVA: Two-way ANOVA is a statistical method used to simultaneously compare means across two independent variables. This approach allows researchers to examine the main effects of each independent variable on a dependent variable and any interaction effects between the two variables. (P. Mishra et al., 2019).For example, imagine a study investigating the effects of teaching methods (with levels such as traditional, online, and interactive) and student study habits (with levels such as regular and irregular) on student performance. In this scenario, the two independent variables are teaching method and study habits, each with multiple levels.

By applying a Two-Way ANOVA, the researcher can assess:
The main effect of the teaching method on test scores.
The main effect of study habits on test scores.
Any interaction effect between teaching method and study habits, which examines whether the student's study habits influence the effectiveness of a teaching method.

If the results yield a p-value below the commonly accepted cutoff of 0.05 for any of these effects, the researcher can conclude that there are significant differences in test scores associated with that factor (or interaction). Furthermore, if there is a significant interaction effect, it suggests that the impact of one independent variable depends on the level of the other independent variable, indicating a more complex relationship between the factors. Two-Way ANOVA is particularly useful in complex experimental designs, as it allows for a more nuanced understanding of how multiple factors and their interactions impact outcomes, enabling researchers to derive richer insights from their data[1].

Post-Hoc Tests: Post-Hoc Tests are statistical analyses conducted after finding significant differences in an ANOVA to determine which specific groups differ from one another. When a researcher identifies a significant effect using ANOVA, it indicates that at least one group mean is different, but it does not specify where those differences lie among the groups (Kim, 2014a).

For example, consider a study that uses One-Way ANOVA to compare average test scores among three teaching methods: traditional, online, and interactive. If the ANOVA results yield a significant p-value, the researcher would then implement post-hoc tests to pinpoint which specific teaching methods result in different mean test scores.

Common post-hoc tests include:

Tukey's HSD (Honestly Significant Difference): This test compares all possible pairs of group means to find which ones are significantly different while controlling for Type I errors (Lane, 2010).

Bonferroni Correction: A more conservative approach that adjusts the significance level based on the number of comparisons made, reducing the risk of finding false positives (Armstrong, 2014).

Scheffé's Test: A versatile test that can be used for various comparisons (not just pairwise), useful if researchers are interested in complex comparisons between groups (Allen, 2017).

Implementing these post-hoc tests provides a clearer picture of the data, allowing researchers to understand the specific differences between groups and draw more informed conclusions about their findings.

4. Chi-Square Tests

Chi-square tests are statistical methods used to assess the relationship between two categorical variables—variables that can be divided into distinct categories without any inherent order. These tests help determine whether there is a significant association between the variables or if any observed differences are due to chance. (Yeager, n.d.).

For example, a researcher may conduct a Chi-square test to examine the relationship between gender (male, female) and preference for a specific type of activity (e.g., sports, arts, and music) among participants. The researcher would collect data on the frequency of each combination of categories (e.g., how many males prefer sports versus how many females prefer sports).

After organising the data into a contingency table, the Chi-square test calculates the expected frequencies assuming no association between the variables. The results yield a p-value indicating whether any observed frequency differences are statistically significant.

If the p-value is below the commonly accepted threshold (typically set at 0.05), the researcher would reject the null hypothesis, concluding that there is a significant relationship between the two categorical variables. Chi-square tests are widely used in various fields, including social sciences, healthcare, and marketing, to explore associations and patterns within categorical data.

Application: Often used to study associations, such as between gender preferences.

Assumptions: Requires data in frequency counts (numbers of occurrences in each category) and mutually exclusive categories (each participant belongs to one category only).

5. Correlation Analysis

Correlation analysis measures the strength and direction of the relationship between two continuous variables—variables that can take any value within a specified range. This statistical technique helps researchers assess how closely related the variables are and whether an increase or decrease in one variable corresponds with changes in the other (De Vos et al., 2005; Yeager, n.d.).

Pearson's r: One of the most common methods for correlation analysis is Pearson's r, which calculates the correlation coefficient for two continuous variables. For instance, a researcher may perform correlation analysis using Pearson's r to examine the relationship between the amount of exercise (measured in hours per week) and cholesterol levels in a group of individuals. Here, both variables are continuous; hours of exercise can range from 0 to whatever maximum is set, and cholesterol levels can vary within a health-related range (Yeager, n.d.).

The result of Pearson's r is a correlation coefficient that ranges from -1 to +1. A coefficient close to +1 indicates a strong positive correlation, meaning that the other variable also tends to increase as one variable increases. Conversely, a coefficient close to -1 indicates a strong negative correlation, suggesting that as one variable increases, the other decreases. A coefficient around 0 implies little to no correlation between the variables (Yeager, n.d.).

Caution: While Pearson's r provides useful insights into the relationship between continuous variables, it is essential to remember that correlation does not imply causation; other factors or variables may influence any observed relationship.

6. Advanced Techniques

Advanced Techniques in statistical analysis provide more sophisticated methods for understanding complex relationships among variables, identifying trends, and reducing data dimensionality. Here are three key techniques:

Structural Equation Modelling (SEM): SEM is a powerful statistical technique that tests complex relationships among multiple variables, including both direct and indirect effects. It allows researchers to build and evaluate theoretical models that represent relationships among observed and latent variables. For instance, SEM can be used to examine how factors such as socio-economic status, educational attainment, and parental involvement can collectively influence student performance (Thakkar, 2020).

Time Series Analysis: This technique analyses data collected over time to identify trends and seasonal effects, which are repeating patterns observed at specific intervals. Time series analysis is often used in fields like economics and environmental science to forecast future values based on historical data. For example, a researcher may analyse monthly sales data for a retail store to identify seasonal trends and predict future sales patterns (Shin, 2017).

Factor Analysis: Factor analysis reduces data dimensionality by identifying underlying latent variables (unobserved factors) that explain correlations among observed variables. This technique is particularly useful when dealing with large datasets containing numerous variables, as it helps to simplify the data without losing significant information (Syed Mohammad, 2009). For instance, a survey measuring consumer preferences might use factor analysis to group related preferences into broader categories, making it easier to interpret and analyse the data.

Hypothetically Analysing Insights; Quantitative Data Analysis at Riverside Academy

Dr Emily initiated a research project at Riverside Academy to understand the factors influencing student success. With a keen focus on quantitative analysis, she recognised that choosing statistical methods would be crucial in drawing meaningful conclusions from her collected data.

Regression Analysis: Establishing Relationships

To begin her investigation, Dr Emily used regression analysis to explore the relationship between student success—measured by academic performance (the dependent variable)—and several predictors, including attendance, study habits, and socio-economic status (independent variables).

She applied linear regression, assuming a straight-line relationship between these variables. By calculating regression coefficients, she estimated the strength and direction of the relationships. A positive coefficient indicated that academic performance improved as attendance increased, while a negative coefficient suggested that poorer study habits were associated with lower performance.

Dr Emily was careful to check the assumptions underpinning her analysis: linearity (ensuring the relationships were indeed linear), independence of errors (ensuring that the differences between actual and predicted values were uncorrelated), and homoscedasticity (constant variance of errors). She understood that violations of these assumptions could lead to inaccurate estimates, so she took time to validate her data before interpreting her results.

t-Tests: Comparing Means

Next, Dr Emily sought to assess whether there were significant differences in academic performance between different groups of students. For this, she conducted t-tests.

First, she used the independent samples t-test to compare the means of academic performance between male and female students. This test helped her determine whether the observed differences were statistically significant. For instance, she found that the average scores for females were higher than those for males, leading her to investigate further.

For groups measured at two different times, such as their scores before and after a particular intervention, Dr Emily applied the paired samples t-test. This allowed her to evaluate whether their academic performance had significantly improved following the programme.

The t-tests provided p-values that indicated the probability of any observed differences occurring by chance. A p-value below 0.05 led Dr Emily to conclude that the differences in performance were statistically significant.

Analysis of Variance (ANOVA): Expanding Comparisons

As her research progressed, Dr Emily realised she needed to compare means across three or more groups—specifically, different teaching methods implemented in the classroom. To do this, she applied ANOVA (Analysis of Variance).

In her study, she conducted a one-way ANOVA, which compared means across one independent variable with multiple levels (different teaching methods). Upon finding significant differences between these teaching approaches, Dr Emily then performed post-hoc tests, such as Tukey's HSD, to identify which specific groups differed from one another.

This method provided a clearer picture of the most effective teaching strategies.

Chi-Square Tests: Exploring Categorical Relationships

Dr Emily also wanted to explore relationships between categorical variables, such as students' extracurricular participation and overall academic performance. For this, she utilised chi-square tests.

This statistical method assessed whether there were significant associations between the two categorical variables. She ensured her data was in frequency counts, allowing her to interpret how different categories affected student engagement. For example, she discovered that students involved in extracurricular activities had higher academic performance, prompting her to examine the reasons behind this correlation.

Correlation Analysis: Measuring the Strength of Relationships

Recognising that relationships between continuous variables, such as homework hours and test scores, were also critical, Dr Emily turned to correlation analysis. She used Pearson's r, which ranges from -1 to +1, to quantify the strength and direction of the relationships.

Dr Emily found a strong positive correlation between the number of homework hours and students' test scores, but she was careful to remind her audience that correlation does not imply causation—just because two variables were linked does not mean that one caused the other.

Advanced Techniques: Delving Deeper

As Dr Emily sought to uncover more complex relationships among multiple variables, she adopted advanced techniques such as Structural Equation Modelling (SEM).

This method allowed her to examine the direct and indirect effects of various predictors on student success, comprehensively analysing interrelated factors.

She also applied time series analysis to identify trends across academic years, observing patterns in enrolment and performance. Moreover, when faced with large datasets, she used factor analysis to reduce dimensionality, identifying underlying factors influencing student outcomes.

Conclusions and Contributions

After completing her analysis, Dr Emily presented the relationships and differences identified through her statistical methods, demonstrating how various teaching methods and student behaviours were associated with academic success.

Her systematic approach to quantitative data analysis highlighted the practical application of different statistical techniques within the positivist research paradigm. Dr Emily's findings showed that attendance and study habits significantly influenced academic performance, indicating a need for targeted interventions in these areas.

Conclusion

Selecting the appropriate quantitative analysis technique is essential for successful positivist research. Each method has its strengths and limitations, and researchers need to understand these factors when choosing statistical methods thoroughly. Furthermore, each technique's assumptions should be considered, as violations can affect validity (accuracy).

Interpreting statistical results requires understanding both their significance (the importance of the results) and practical implications. Effect sizes, which measure relationships' magnitude (size), complement p-values by providing context. A statistically significant finding with a small effect size may lack practical relevance.

Hence, employing suitable quantitative data analysis techniques is vital for positivist research. These techniques are part of the broader statistical toolkit available to social scientists. Mastery of these methods enables researchers to derive meaningful insights, contributing to our understanding of social phenomena. The ongoing development of statistical methods continues to enhance researchers' abilities to navigate the complexities of the social world, affirming that effective analysis is a key component of robust scientific practice.

Table 7: Quantitative Data Analysis Techniques

Technique	Description	Key Points
Regression Analysis	Examines the relationship between a dependent variable and one or more independent variables.	- **Linear Regression**: Assumes a straight-line relationships - **Assumptions**: Checks for linearity and errors.
t-Tests	Compares the means of two groups to identify significant differences.	- **Independent Samples t-Test**: Compares means from two independent groups. - **Paired Samples t-Test**: Compares means from the same group at two different times.
Analysis of Variance (ANOVA)	Compares means across three or more groups to determine if at least one group mean differs significantly.	- **One-Way ANOVA**: For one independent variable with multiple levels. - **Two-Way ANOVA**: For two or more independent variables. - **Post-Hoc Tests**: Identify which groups differ.
Chi-Square Tests	Assesses the relationship between two categorical variables.	- Evaluates frequency counts in categories (e.g., gender and voting preferences).
Correlation Analysis	Measures the strength and direction of a linear relationship between two continuous variables.	- **Pearson's r**: Ranges from -1 to +1; indicates the strength of correlation. - Caution: Correlation does not imply causation.
Advanced Techniques	Includes methods for complex analyses and data exploration.	- **Structural Equation Modelling (SEM)**: Tests relationships among multiple variables. - **Time Series Analysis**: Studies patterns in data over time. - **Factor Analysis**: Reduces data dimensionality by identifying latent variables.

VALIDITY AND RELIABILITY IN POSITIVIST RESEARCH

Understanding validity and reliability is essential for ensuring rigorous research. These concepts assess the trustworthiness and generalisability of research findings, ensuring that conclusions accurately reflect the studied phenomena (Heale & Twycross, 2015).

1. Internal Validity

Internal validity refers to the extent to which observed effects in a study can be confidently attributed to the independent variable rather than to external factors or confounding variables.

High internal validity indicates that the study's design and implementation effectively control for alternative explanations, allowing researchers to make strong causal inferences about the relationship between the independent and dependent variables (Patino & Ferreira, 2018).

For example, in an experiment examining the effect of a new teaching method on student performance, high internal validity would mean that any observed improvement in test scores can be confidently attributed to the teaching method itself, rather than to other factors such as prior knowledge, differences in student motivation, or external classroom conditions.

Key points include:

Confounding Variables: Extraneous factors can obscure the true relationship between variables, potentially biasing study results (De Vos et al., 2005).

For example, if a study examines the effect of a new educational programme on student performance without accounting for students' prior knowledge, the results may not accurately reflect the programme's effectiveness.

Mitigation Strategies:

Random Assignment: Randomly assigning participants to different groups helps ensure comparability at the start of the study. This is important because it reduces systematic differences between groups that could influence the outcome. For instance, if one group had a higher baseline knowledge level than another, it would skew the results (Rutkowski et al., 2024). Random assignment helps establish that any observed outcome differences can be more confidently attributed to the treatment rather than pre-existing differences among participants.

Statistical Control: Techniques such as multiple regression can account for confounding variables, isolating the effect of the independent variable by statistically controlling for other influencing factors. This approach allows researchers to delineate the relationship being studied with greater clarity, providing a more accurate picture of how the independent variable impacts the dependent variable (Handley et al., 2018).

2. External Validity

External validity assesses the generalisability of findings to other populations and settings. Key considerations include (Patino & Ferreira, 2018):

Sampling Bias: If the sample does not accurately represent the population, results may not be applicable elsewhere (Busetto et al., 2020). For instance, studying a new therapy using only university students may not apply to the general population, as older adults may have different responses due to age-related factors.

Context Factors: The specific environment where the research is conducted can limit applicability. Results from a controlled lab setting may differ from real-world settings due to differing influences (Cook et al., 2023).

Strategies for Enhancing External Validity:

Strategies for Enhancing External Validity aim to ensure that research findings can be generalised to a broader population and applied in various contexts. Key strategies include:

1. Researchers should aim to include diverse samples that represent various demographics, such as age, gender, ethnicity, socio-economic status, and other relevant characteristics. By ensuring that the sample reflects the diversity of the larger population, the findings become more applicable to a broader audience. For instance, if a study on an educational programme primarily includes students from a single socio-economic background, the results may not be generalisable to students from different backgrounds.

2. By conducting research in various settings, researchers can test whether the findings hold true across different contexts. This might involve replicating a study in different schools, communities, or geographical locations. If the results are consistent across these various settings, it enhances the credibility of the findings and suggests that the conclusions can be generalised beyond the specific circumstances of the original study. For example, an educational intervention that proves effective in urban schools should also be tested in rural schools to confirm its broader applicability.

3. Reliability

Reliability refers to the consistency of a measure over time and across different observers. Key types include (Vilagut, 2014):

Test-Retest Reliability: Assesses consistency over time (Vilagut, 2014). For example, a questionnaire measuring anxiety should yield similar scores for the same individual when taken weeks apart. This consistency is crucial for demonstrating that the measure is stable over time.

Inter-Rater Reliability: Evaluates agreement between different observers measuring the same phenomenon (Gwet, 2014). For instance, if two researchers code behaviours during an observation study, a high agreement indicates that the measure is reliable, as different observers interpret the phenomenon similarly.

Internal Consistency: Checks whether items within a measure produce similar results. A reliable scale should yield consistent scores across its items (Revicki, 2014). For example, if a scale measures happiness, all questions designed to assess happiness should produce similar scores for the same participant.

4. Addressing Reliability Threats

Threats to reliability can arise from measurement errors, such as poorly designed instruments or inconsistent administration (Vilagut, 2014):

Example: An experiment measuring stress levels conducted at different times of day could yield varying results due to differences in participants' alertness. Ensuring consistent conditions during measurement helps mitigate this risk.

Strategies for Improvement:

Use well-validated measures and clearly defined variables. This helps ensure that what is being measured truly reflects the concept of interest. Employ standardised procedures for administering assessments. Consistency in how measures are taken enhances reliability.

Conduct pilot testing to identify and fix potential problems before conducting the main study.

5. The Interplay of Validity and Reliability

Both validity and reliability are essential for sound research. A study can be reliable (yielding consistent results) but not valid (not accurately measuring what it claims) (Heale & Twycross, 2015). For instance, a scale that measures something other than happiness can be consistent in its responses but not valid for measuring happiness (Heale & Twycross, 2015).

Conversely, a measure can be valid (accurately reflecting the phenomenon) but not reliable (producing inconsistent results). **Validity and reliability should coexist, contributing to trustworthy findings**. Researchers should strive to maximise both qualities to generate meaningful and generalisable knowledge (Heale & Twycross, 2015).

Example One: Ensuring Rigour; Validity and Reliability in Dr Lisa's Social Sciences Research

At Bramblewood University, Dr Lisa, a social sciences researcher, initiated a study investigating the impact of a new mentorship programme on student retention and academic success. Recognising that the integrity of her findings depended on the concepts of validity and reliability, she carefully designed her research to address these crucial elements from the beginning.

Internal Validity: Establishing Confidence in Results

To ensure internal validity, Dr Lisa focused on linking observed effects specifically to the mentorship programme rather than external factors. She recognised that confounding variables could obscure the relationship between her independent variable (the mentorship programme) and her dependent variable (student retention and success).

For instance, she understood that results could be biased if students' prior academic achievements were not accounted for. To mitigate this risk, she implemented random assignment, placing students into either the mentorship or control group randomly. This approach helped ensure comparability at the start of the study, reducing systematic differences that could influence outcomes. For example, if one group possessed inherently higher academic ability, it could skew the results. Dr Lisa also applied statistical control techniques, such as multiple regression analysis, to account for any confounding variables. By isolating the effects of the mentorship programme, she aimed to understand its impact on student success.

External Validity: Generalising Findings Across Populations

Dr Lisa focused on external validity as her research progressed, assessing how her findings could be generalised to other populations and settings. She was aware of potential sampling bias; if her sample did not accurately represent the broader student population, her results may not be applicable elsewhere.

For example, if she only studied students from one specific programme, the outcomes may not reflect students' experiences in varied educational contexts. To address this concern, Dr Lisa ensured that her sample included a diverse range of students from different backgrounds and demographics. She also conducted her study in multiple settings—across various universities—to validate whether her findings held true outside her initial research environment. This enhanced the generalisability of her results.

Reliability: Ensuring Consistency in Measurements

Understanding that dependability was crucial, Dr Lisa focused on reliability. She needed to ensure her research instruments consistently measured their intended constructs. To assess test-retest reliability, she administered her measures (such as questionnaires assessing student engagement) to the same participants at two different time points. This allowed her to check whether the responses remained stable over time. If students' scores were comparable weeks apart, it indicated that her measure was reliable.

Inter-rater reliability was also important. When multiple observers evaluated students' engagement in the mentorship programme, she ensured that their judgements aligned. By training her research assistants thoroughly and comparing their assessments, Dr Lisa confirmed a high level of agreement, reinforcing the reliability of her observational data.

Addressing Threats to Reliability

Dr Lisa was mindful that measurement errors could threaten reliability. For instance, she considered how variations in stress levels may affect assessments. To mitigate this risk, she standardised the conditions during measurements, ensuring that all assessments took place under similar circumstances.

She also used well-validated measures, ensuring that her instruments accurately reflected the concepts being studied. Additionally, conducting pilot tests helped identify potential issues before the main study commenced, refining her instruments for clarity and precision.

The Interplay of Validity and Reliability

Throughout her research journey, Dr Lisa recognised the important relationship between validity and reliability. She understood that a study could produce consistent results without being valid—meaning it could measure the wrong construct. For example, if a scale claimed to measure student engagement but instead tapped into unrelated factors, it could yield reliable but misleading conclusions. Conversely, a measure could be valid yet unreliable, yielding inconsistent results over time.

Dr Lisa aimed to enhance both aspects, ensuring her findings were trustworthy and relevant. She believed that achieving high validity and reliability would contribute to the depth of knowledge in the social sciences.

Summary: The Path to Credible Research

After completing her research, Dr Lisa presented her findings to colleagues at Bramblewood University. She demonstrated how the mentorship programme significantly influenced student retention and academic success, attributing these effects to the quality of the mentorship.

Her commitment to maintaining validity and reliability throughout her research strengthened the credibility of her findings. By addressing threats to internal and external validity and ensuring the reliability of her measures, Dr Lisa formulated rigorous conclusions applicable to broader educational contexts.

Dr Lisa's research highlighted the importance of a comprehensive approach to research design. By prioritising accurate and consistent measurements, she provided insights to the university and encouraged fellow researchers to uphold these standards in their work, furthering the understanding of social phenomena.

Example Two: Hypothetically Navigating Challenges; Limitations of Positivist Research in Sociological Studies

Dr Martin was conducting a research project at Greenwood University to evaluate the effectiveness of a new educational programme designed to improve student engagement and academic performance. While the positivist framework offered a solid foundation for his study, Dr Martin was acutely aware of the limitations and challenges inherent in this approach.

Internal Validity: Ensuring Accurate Attribution of Effects

As Dr Martin delved into his research, he recognised the importance of internal validity—the extent to which he could confidently attribute observed effects to the independent variable rather than to external factors. He knew that confounding variables—uncontrolled outside factors—could obscure true relationships.

For instance, if he neglected to control for students' prior knowledge or academic performance, any observed improvement could reflect existing differences rather than the programme's effectiveness. Dr Martin employed random assignment to mitigate these risks, ensuring that participant characteristics were evenly distributed between the experimental and control groups. This method helped reduce bias and strengthened the validity of his findings.

Additionally, he utilised statistical control methods, such as multiple regression analysis, to account for potential confounding variables. By isolating the impact of the educational programme, Dr Martin aimed to obtain a clearer understanding of its effectiveness.

External Validity: Challenges in Generalisation

Next, Dr Martin focused on external validity, assessing whether his findings could be generalised beyond his specific study group. He was mindful of sampling bias; his findings may not apply more broadly if his sample were not representative of the broader student population—such as relying solely on university students for a programme aimed at a wider demographic.

Moreover, context factors posed additional challenges. The research environment could limit the applicability of the results; outcomes obtained from a tightly controlled laboratory setting could differ significantly from those in real-world educational contexts. Dr Martin aimed to recruit a diverse sample across different demographics to enhance external validity and conduct the study in various educational settings.

Reliability: Ensuring Consistency in Findings

Recognising that reliability was just as critical as validity, Dr Martin focused on ensuring the consistency of his research findings. He considered different types of reliability, including test-retest reliability, which checks for consistency over time. For example, the anxiety questionnaire administered before and after the programme should yield similar scores for the same individuals.

Additionally, inter-rater reliability was essential when multiple observers assessed student engagement during classroom activities. Dr Martin trained his research assistants thoroughly, ensuring that their coding of behaviours reflected a high level of agreement, thus reinforcing the reliability of his observational data.

Dr Martin employed well-validated measures and standardised procedures to address potential reliability issues and minimise measurement errors. He understood that consistent conditions during data collection were vital for enhancing reliability.

The Interplay of Validity and Reliability

Dr Martin remained conscious of the interplay between validity and reliability throughout his research process. He recognised that while a measurement could be reliable—yielding consistent results —it may not accurately capture what it was intended to measure. For example, a scale that purported to measure happiness could instead reflect life satisfaction if not carefully designed.

Summary: Acknowledging the Limitations

After completing his research and analysing the data, Dr Martin presented his findings to his colleagues at Greenwood University. He emphasised the importance of acknowledging and addressing the limitations of positivist research. While he had achieved robust evidence for the causal relationships examined, he recognised challenges such as striving for complete objectivity, ensuring valid generalisations, and managing potential biases.

From his experiences, Dr Martin outlined strategies for enhancing the quality of positivist research: rigorous research design, careful data collection, and critical self-awareness of biases. He encouraged his peers to integrate various research methods and maintain transparency in their studies.

Ultimately, Dr Martin's work demonstrated that a balanced approach, recognising both the strengths and limitations of positivism, is essential for advancing social science research. By acknowledging these challenges, researchers could contribute valuable insights to our understanding of social phenomena, driving the sociology field forward with rigour and integrity.

Table 8: Summary of Positivist Concepts

Aspect	Description
1. Internal Validity	Refers to how well researchers can confidently attribute observed effects to independent variables instead of external factors.
Confounding Variables	Extraneous factors that can obscure true relationships. For example, not accounting for students' prior knowledge in an educational study may bias results.
Mitigation Strategies	- Random Assignment: Ensures participant characteristics are evenly distributed. - Statistical Control: Adjusts for the influence of confounding variables.
2. External Validity	Assesses whether findings can be generalised to other populations or settings.
Sampling Bias	Occurs when the sample is not representative of the population, limiting the applicability of results (e.g., only using university students for a therapy study).
Context Factors	The research setting can affect the results. Outcomes from a controlled lab may differ from real-world environments.
3. Reliability	Measures the consistency of research findings.
Types of Reliability	- Test-Retest Reliability: Consistency over time (e.g., similar scores on an anxiety questionnaire weeks apart). - Inter-Rater Reliability: Agreement between different observers.
Addressing Reliability Issues	Use well-validated measures and standardised procedures to minimise measurement errors.

Conclusion

In conclusion, pursuing validity and reliability is integral to the success of positivist research. Researchers enhance the credibility and applicability of their findings by addressing threats to internal and external validity and ensuring the reliability of measures. Understanding these concepts is crucial for conducting rigorous research that contributes to knowledge in the social sciences.

The interplay between validity and reliability highlights the need for a holistic approach to research design. By ensuring accurate and consistent measurements, researchers can provide findings that are not only reliable but also relevant to broader societal issues and contexts. Rigorous attention to validity and reliability helps create a robust body of knowledge that advances our understanding of social phenomena.

CHAPTER 3: POST-POSITIVIST RESEARCH DESIGNS

QUALITATIVE RESEARCH METHODS IN THE POST-POSITIVIST FRAMEWORK

Qualitative research methods offer a valuable alternative to the quantitative approaches typical in the positivist paradigm. While positivism concentrates on numerical data and objective measurements, qualitative research seeks to provide a deeper understanding of complex social phenomena by exploring individuals' experiences, perspectives, and meanings (Bazen et al., 2021). This shift highlights the post-positivist recognition of the inherent subjectivity in research and the limitations of solely relying on quantifiable data to capture human experiences. Several distinct approaches fall under qualitative research, each with its unique strengths and challenges.

Key Qualitative Research Approaches

1. Ethnography

Ethnography is a qualitative research method where researchers immerse themselves in a particular culture or social group to gain an insider's perspective (Kramer & Adams, 2017). This enables a deep understanding of the group's practices, beliefs, and social dynamics (Kramer & Adams, 2017).

Example: A researcher studying a community's approach to mental health could live there for several months, observing daily life, participating in community events, and interviewing residents about their beliefs and practices related to mental health. This immersive experience allows the researcher to gather rich, nuanced insights into the community's social dynamics and cultural norms.

Strengths: Ethnography produces rich, contextualised data that captures the complexity of social interactions. The in-depth engagement with participants leads to a comprehensive understanding of how cultural and social factors influence behaviours and beliefs.

Limitations: However, it is time-consuming and can be influenced by the researcher's biases, which may affect data interpretation. This emphasises the need for reflexivity—self-awareness of one's influence on the research process and findings—which is crucial for enhancing the credibility and validity of the research outcomes.

2. Grounded Theory

Grounded Theory aims to develop new theories based on empirical data rather than testing existing theories (Delmas & Giles, 2022). This qualitative research methodology focuses on generating theories that emerge directly from the data collected during the research process (Delmas & Giles, 2022).

Example: A researcher interested in the experiences of individuals coping with chronic illness might conduct interviews with patients to gather data about their daily lives and challenges. They would systematically code the responses to identify recurring themes, leading to the development of a theory regarding how individuals manage their health. This process could uncover new coping strategies that had not been previously recognised in the literature.

Strengths: Grounded theory generates novel theories that are directly rooted in real experiences, providing a framework for understanding complex social phenomena.

Limitations: However, grounded theory can be time-intensive, requiring researchers to engage in repetitive cycles of data collection and analysis. This method also demands significant analytical skills to effectively identify patterns and develop coherent theories from the data.

3. Phenomenology

Phenomenology focuses on understanding the lived experiences of individuals and the essence of specific phenomena (Delmas & Giles, 2022).

Example: A researcher could explore the phenomenon of grief by conducting in-depth interviews with individuals who have recently lost loved ones. The aim is to uncover common themes in their emotional experiences, such as feelings of isolation or the process of finding support from friends and family.

Strengths: Provides deep insights into how people construct meaning from their experiences.

Limitations: Small sample sizes can limit the generalisability of findings.

4. Case Studies

Case studies involve an in-depth examination of a single case, group, event, or situation (Delmas & Giles, 2022).

Example: A case study may focus on a specific school implementing a new educational programme, gathering data from interviews with teachers, observations of classrooms, and analysing student performance data. This comprehensive approach allows for a detailed understanding of the factors influencing the programme's success.

Strengths: Offers rich, contextual insights into complex issues.

Limitations: Findings may lack generalisability to other contexts or populations.

5. Surveys (Qualitative)

Qualitative surveys collect narrative data through open-ended questions that allow participants to express their thoughts in detail (Braun, Clarke, Boulton, Davey, & McEvoy, 2021).

Example: A researcher investigating the impact of social media on self-esteem may design a survey with open-ended questions, allowing adolescents to describe how social media affects their feelings about themselves.

Strengths: Captures comprehensive qualitative data that reflects participants' experiences.

Limitations: Analyzing qualitative survey data can be complex and time-consuming.

Data Collection Techniques

Interviews: Researchers conduct structured (set questions) or unstructured (flexible and exploratory) interviews to gather detailed narratives (Bazen et al., 2021). Example: An unstructured interview with a participant discussing their journey with a chronic illness may yield rich details about their coping mechanisms and support systems.

Focus Groups: Group discussions on a specific topic can reveal shared beliefs and diverse perspectives (Creaven & Kirwan, 2024). Example: A focus group with students discussing their experiences with online learning may provide insights into both the benefits and challenges they face.

Participant Observation: Researchers engage with and observe a group to collect firsthand data on behaviours in natural settings (Bazen et al., 2021). Example: A researcher observing a support group may note the interactions between members and how they offer support to one another.

Data Analysis

Qualitative data analysis is an iterative process that involves several steps (Bazen et al., 2021):

Transcribing: Converting recorded interviews or focus groups into written text for analysis (Busetto et al., 2020).

Coding: Identifying key themes and patterns in the data (Busetto et al., 2020). For example, coding could reveal that several participants mention the importance of family support during their grieving process.

Thematic Analysis: This method focuses on identifying, analysing, and reporting patterns (themes) within the data, helping researchers understand the broader implications of their findings (Kramer & Adams, 2017).

Evaluation Criteria

Qualitative researchers use criteria that reflect the nuances of their methods and findings (Swift, 2022):

Credibility: Refers to the trustworthiness of the findings. Researchers may enhance credibility by using triangulation, which involves collecting data from multiple sources or using different methods to confirm results (Korstjens & Moser, 2017).

Transferability: This assesses the extent to which findings can be applied to other contexts or populations. Researchers can provide rich descriptions of the research context to help others determine if the findings are relevant to their own situations (Korstjens & Moser, 2017).

Dependability: This refers to the consistency of findings over time and across researchers. Maintaining detailed documentation throughout the research process can enhance dependability by providing a clear trail of how conclusions were reached (Korstjens & Moser, 2017).

Confirmability: Concerned with whether the findings are based on the data rather than the researcher's biases. Researchers can focus on ensuring that their interpretations are well-supported by the data collected (Korstjens & Moser, 2017).

Hypothetically Exploring A Case Study in Post-Positivist Research Design

At Larkhill University, Dr Fiona initiated a research project to understand the impact of social media on adolescents' self-esteem. Recognising the limitations of quantitative approaches, she chose to adopt qualitative research methods within a post-positivist framework to capture the complex experiences of her participants.

Qualitative Research Methods: A Different Lens

Dr Fiona understood that qualitative research provided an alternative, allowing for a deeper exploration of individuals' experiences and perspectives. While positivist methods focus on numerical data and objective measurements, qualitative approaches offer insights that reflect the subjective realities of social phenomena.

Key Qualitative Research Approaches

Ethnography: To gain an insider's perspective, Dr Fiona considered using ethnography as her primary method. She planned to immerse herself in the community of adolescents she aimed to study, spending several months participating in their daily lives, observing their interactions, and interviewing them about their experiences with social media. This approach promised to yield rich, contextual data that captured the complexity of their social dynamics. However, Dr Fiona recognised that this method was time-consuming and could be influenced by her own biases, highlighting the necessity of maintaining reflexivity throughout the research process.

Grounded Theory: In addition to ethnography, Dr Fiona was drawn to grounded theory, which focuses on generating new theories directly from empirical data rather than testing existing ones. She envisioned conducting in-depth interviews with adolescents to understand their interactions with social media. By coding the responses to identify recurring themes, she aimed to develop a theory regarding how social media impacts their self-esteem, potentially revealing new coping strategies that had not been previously recognised. While this method facilitated the emergence of new theories based on lived experiences, she recognised that its iterative nature could be time-intensive and required strong analytical skills.

Phenomenology: Another approach that interested Dr Fiona was phenomenology, which seeks to understand individuals' lived experiences. She considered investigating the phenomenon of social media distress by conducting interviews with adolescents who had expressed feelings of low self-esteem related to their online presence. Her goal was to uncover common emotional themes, such as feelings of isolation or the quest for validation.

While phenomenology provided insights into how individuals construct meaning from their experiences, Dr Fiona acknowledged that the smaller sample sizes typical of this method could limit the generalisability of her findings.

Case Studies: Dr Fiona contemplated employing case studies, which involve a comprehensive examination of a single case, group, event, or situation. For instance, she could focus on a specific school implementing a programme promoting healthy social media use, gathering data from interviews with students, educators, and parents while analysing related outcomes. This approach offered significant insights into the complexities of the situation but posed the challenge that findings may not generalise to other schools or contexts.

Qualitative Surveys: Dr Fiona planned to conduct qualitative surveys to supplement her research, collecting narrative data through open-ended questions. This would allow adolescents to describe how social media affects their self-esteem. For example, she may ask participants to describe their feelings about their online experiences in their own words. This method could capture detailed and diverse qualitative data, though she recognised that analysing such information could be complex and time-consuming.

Data Collection Techniques

To gather qualitative data, Dr Fiona employed various data collection techniques:

Interviews: She planned to use both structured and unstructured interviews to gather detailed narratives from participants. An unstructured interview with adolescents discussing their social media experiences would yield in-depth insights into their coping mechanisms and support systems.

Focus Groups: Group discussions on topics related to social media effects could reveal shared beliefs and diverse perspectives. Dr Fiona organised a focus group with students to discuss their online experiences, collecting insights into the benefits and challenges they faced.

Participant Observation: Engaging with adolescents during online and offline activities, Dr Fiona intended to observe their behaviours in natural settings to enhance her understanding of their social interactions.

Data Analysis and Evaluation Criteria

Qualitative data analysis involved an iterative process that included transcribing recorded interviews and focus groups into written text for analysis. Dr Fiona applied coding to identify key themes and patterns in the data, allowing her to report on findings effectively. For example, coding could reveal that several participants mentioned the importance of peer support in managing self-esteem. To assess the credibility of her findings, Dr Fiona focused on several evaluation criteria:

Credibility: She aimed to enhance the trustworthiness of her findings through triangulation, drawing data from multiple sources to confirm results.

Transferability: Dr Fiona assessed how her findings could be applied to other contexts or populations. She provided rich, detailed descriptions of her research context, allowing others to evaluate the relevance of the findings to their own situations.

Dependability: Dr Fiona maintained thorough documentation throughout her research process to ensure the consistency of her findings over time and across researchers. This record provided a clear trail detailing how conclusions were reached and enhanced.

Confirmability: Dr Fiona also emphasised the importance of confirmability, which pertains to whether her findings were based on the data rather than her biases. She prioritised ensuring that her interpretations were well-supported by the data collected and engaged in reflexive practices to challenge her assumptions.

Summary: A Holistic Approach to Understanding Individual Experiences

After several months of data collection and analysis, Dr Fiona synthesised her findings, revealing how social media affected adolescents' self-esteem in complex and multifaceted ways. Her research illustrated the diverse narratives of her participants, highlighting both the negative impacts and effective coping strategies they employed.

In her presentation to colleagues at Larkhill University, Dr Fiona discussed how qualitative research methods within the post-positivist framework enabled her to uncover deeper insights into the lived experiences of adolescents. By prioritising subjective accounts and reflections, she demonstrated the value of qualitative approaches in understanding social phenomena. Dr Fiona's work underscored the significance of integrating multiple research methods to understand human experiences comprehensively. She encouraged her peers to acknowledge and incorporate qualitative research into their studies, fostering a richer dialogue about the complexities of social issues.

Through her focus on the nuances of adolescent experiences, Dr Fiona contributed valuable insights to the field of social sciences, paving the way for future research endeavours that prioritise the voices and perspectives of individuals.

Conclusion

In summary, qualitative research methods are crucial within the post-positivist framework, offering deep insights into human experiences. Each approach, whether ethnography, grounded theory, phenomenology, or case studies, brings unique strengths and challenges to the research process. Researchers can comprehensively understand complex social phenomena by thoughtfully selecting the appropriate qualitative approach based on the research question and employing rigorous data collection and analysis techniques. Integrating qualitative and quantitative methods in mixed-methods research exemplifies a flexible and robust strategy for addressing intricate research questions. A nuanced understanding of qualitative research allows for a richer exploration of the social world, reinforcing the importance of diverse research strategies in advancing knowledge.

Table 9: Summary of Qualitative Research Approaches

Aspect	Details
Definition	Qualitative research methods provide an alternative to quantitative approaches by exploring experiences, perspectives, and meanings.
Key Approaches	**Ethnography** Immerses the researcher in a culture or group for deep insights. Example: Living in a community to study mental health practices. **Grounded Theory** Develops theories based on empirical data through iterative analysis. Example: Interviewing chronic illness patients to identify common coping strategies. **Phenomenology** Focuses on understanding individual lived experiences. Example: Inquiring into grief experiences after losing a loved one. **Case Studies** Provides in-depth analysis of a specific case or phenomenon. Example: Investigating a school's implementation of a new curriculum. **Surveys** (Qualitative) Collects open-ended responses to gather narrative data.
Data Collection Technique	- **Interviews**: Gather narratives from structured or unstructured formats. - **Focus Groups:** Group discussions reveal shared beliefs. - **Participant Observation:** Direct engagement in the group being studied.
Data Analysis	An iterative process involving: - **Transcribing**: Turning recordings into written data. - **Coding:** Identifying themes and patterns. - **Thematic Analysis:** Examining patterns to draw conclusions.
Evaluation Criteria	- **Credibility:** Trustworthiness of findings. - **Transferability:** Applicability of findings to other contexts. - **Dependability:** Consistency over time. - **Confirmability:** Findings grounded in data without researcher bias.

DATA COLLECTION TECHNIQUES IN QUALITATIVE RESEARCH WITHIN THE POST-POSITIVIST FRAMEWORK

Qualitative research relies on carefully collecting detailed data that captures the complexities of human experiences. Unlike quantitative research, which focuses on numerical data, qualitative research seeks to understand perspectives, beliefs, and behaviours in natural settings. The choice of data collection methods is crucial and depends on the research question and available resources. Below are key techniques commonly used in qualitative research (Shannon-Baker, 2023).

1. Interviews

Interviews are a primary method for gathering qualitative data, ranging from structured to unstructured formats (Bazen et al., 2021).

Structured Interviews: Involve a set list of predetermined questions, ensuring consistency across participants. This method allows for easier comparison but may limit depth (Busetto et al., 2020). **Example**: A structured interview may ask participants to rate their satisfaction with a service on a scale, providing quantifiable data.

Unstructured Interviews: Open conversations enable deeper exploration of participants' thoughts and feelings (Roos, van der Westhuizen, & Keyter, 2016). **Example**: An unstructured interview could explore a participant's experience with mental health by asking broad questions like, "Can you tell me about your journey with anxiety?"

Semi-Structured Interviews: Combine structure with flexibility, using an interview guide that covers key themes while allowing for follow-up questions based on responses (Busetto et al., 2020).

Example: A researcher may use a semi-structured interview to explore how individuals cope with chronic pain, allowing participants to share their unique coping strategies while ensuring key topics are covered.

2. Focus Groups

Focus groups bring together a small group of participants to discuss a specific topic, allowing for rich dialogue and interaction (Bazen et al., 2021). **Example**: A focus group could explore community attitudes towards a new health initiative, revealing participants' differing opinions and shared beliefs.

Challenges: Managing group dynamics is essential, as some participants may dominate the conversation while others may be reluctant to speak. The researcher should create a safe and respectful environment for all voices to be heard.

3. Observation

Observation involves systematically watching and documenting behaviour in natural settings (Denzin & Lincoln, 2004).

Participant Observation: The researcher actively engages with the group being studied to gather firsthand insights into daily interactions and social dynamics (Busetto et al., 2020).

Example: A researcher may observe a classroom to understand student-teacher interactions and how they affect learning.

Non-Participant Observation: The researcher remains detached to observe without interfering, which can provide a more objective perspective. However, this approach may limit the depth of understanding (Busetto et al., 2020).

Be Aware of The Hawthorne Effect

The Hawthorne Effect refers to the phenomenon where individuals alter their behaviour in response to being observed or studied. This concept originated from a series of studies conducted in the 1920s and 1930s at the Hawthorne Works factory in Chicago, where researchers aimed to examine the relationship between working conditions and productivity ("Hawthorne Effect Definition: How It Works and Is It Real," n.d.).

Key Characteristics:

Awareness of Observation: The Hawthorne Effect occurs when individuals recognise that they are part of a study, leading them to modify their behaviour, often resulting in increased productivity or performance

(Gillespie, 2003).

Temporary Change: The changes in behaviour are typically temporary and may revert to baseline levels once the observation ends or the individual is no longer aware of being studied (Gillespie, 2003).

Implications for Research: This effect highlights the importance of considering how observational methods can impact data collection. Researchers need to account for potential biases introduced by participants' awareness of being observed, especially in settings like educational or workplace studies (Gillespie, 2003).

To minimise the Hawthorne Effect, researchers can:

Use unobtrusive observation methods to reduce participants' awareness of the study. Conduct baseline measurements before participants are informed about the study. Ensure a comfortable environment to alleviate participants' pressure from being observed.

Understanding the Hawthorne Effect is crucial for researchers to enhance the validity of their findings and interpret results accurately in studies involving human behaviour (Gillespie, 2003).

4. Document Analysis

Document analysis examines existing documents, such as reports, diaries, and social media posts, to glean insights into social phenomena (Busetto et al., 2020). **Example**: A researcher studying social movements could analyse activist pamphlets and letters to understand the movement's ideologies and strategies.

Considerations: It's essential to evaluate the quality of documents and recognise potential biases, as documents may not always provide objective representations.

5. Mixed Methods

Many qualitative studies benefit from using a mixed-methods approach, combining various techniques for comprehensive data collection (Braun et al., 2021). **Example**: A study on chronic illness may include semi-structured interviews for rich personal insights, focus groups to discuss coping strategies, and document analysis of health records to gather additional context.

This combination enhances the validity and reliability of findings through triangulation (using multiple methods to validate results).

Ethical Considerations

Ethical considerations are paramount when selecting data collection methods (Lobmeier, 2010):

Informed Consent: Participants should understand the **purpose** of the research and provide consent voluntarily (Kaufman & Ramarao, 2005).

Anonymity and Confidentiality: Researchers should ensure participants' identities are protected (Kaufman & Ramarao, 2005). For example, no identifying details are used when collecting data.

Minimising Harm: It is crucial to safeguard participants from potential risks associated with the study (Kaufman & Ramarao, 2005) for instance, be mindful of traumatic events that could affect participants.

Community Sensitivity: Researchers should be mindful of the broader impact of their research on the communities involved (Kaufman & Ramarao, 2005).

Table 10: Ethical Considerations

Consideration	Description
Informed Consent	Participants should understand the purpose and agree to participate voluntarily.
Anonymity and Confidentiality	Ensuring that participants' identities are protected throughout the study.
Minimising Harm	Safeguarding participants from potential risks associated with the research.
Community Sensitivity	Being mindful of the broader impact of research on the communities involved.

Hypothetical Example of Capturing Complexity; Data Collection Techniques in Qualitative Research

Dr Samira at Willowbrook University initiated a project to explore the experiences of individuals with chronic illness. Recognising the limitations of quantitative methods, she opted for qualitative research to capture the complexity of human experiences. Understanding that the choice of data collection methods was critical to her project's success, she carefully selected techniques that aligned with her research questions and available resources.

1. Interviews: A Pathway to Depth

Dr Samira commenced her research with interviews as a primary method for gathering qualitative data. She utilised various formats to suit different contexts and objectives. Structured interviews involved a predetermined set of questions to ensure consistency across participants. This method allowed her to collect comparable data but may limit the depth of responses.

For example, she may ask participants to rate their satisfaction with healthcare services on a scale, yielding quantifiable data useful for analysis.

Dr Samira also conducted unstructured interviews to explore participants' thoughts and feelings more freely. For instance, she asked, "Can you tell me about your journey with chronic illness?" This approach enabled participants to share their narratives, providing detailed insights into their experiences.

Additionally, Dr Samira utilised semi-structured interviews, combining the advantages of both structured and unstructured formats. With an interview guide focusing on key themes, she allowed for flexibility with follow-up questions. For example, while discussing coping mechanisms with individuals managing chronic pain, she encouraged them to share their unique strategies while addressing essential topics.

2. Focus Groups: Engaging Dialogue

Dr Samira organised focus groups to facilitate discussions among participants around specific topics. By convening a small group of individuals living with chronic illness, she fostered dialogue about their shared experiences and perspectives.

For example, a focus group may explore community attitudes towards a new health initiative, revealing participants' differing opinions and shared beliefs. Managing group dynamics was challenging; some individuals may dominate the discussion while others remained reticent. Dr Samira aimed to create an environment conducive to participation, encouraging all voices to be heard.

3. Observation: Firsthand Insights

Dr Samira implemented observation as a data collection technique, systematically documenting behaviour in natural settings.

She engaged in participant observation, gathering firsthand insights into daily interactions and social dynamics by observing support groups for individuals with chronic illnesses. In contrast, she conducted non-participant observation in clinical settings, where her presence allowed for a more objective perspective. While this method could limit the depth of understanding, it enabled her to explore interactions between healthcare professionals and patients without influencing the dynamics.

4. Document Analysis: Exploring Existing Narratives

To complement her primary data, Dr Samira employed document analysis, examining existing materials such as patients' diaries, healthcare reports, and social media posts. By analysing these documents, she aimed to glean insights into the narratives surrounding chronic illness.

For instance, studying activist pamphlets and letters related to healthcare advocacy helped her understand broader social movements and their impact. Dr Samira evaluated the quality of these documents and acknowledged potential biases, recognising that they could not provide entirely objective representations of experiences.

5. Mixed Methods: A Comprehensive Approach

Understanding the strengths and limitations of individual methods, Dr Samira recognised the benefits of a mixed-methods approach. By combining various techniques, she aimed to gather comprehensive data to enrich her findings.

For example, her study on chronic illness included semi-structured interviews to gain personal insights, focus groups to discuss coping strategies, and document analysis of health records to provide additional context. This triangulation of methods enhanced the validity and reliability of her findings, ensuring a more robust understanding of the participants' lived experiences.

Ethical Considerations: Safeguarding Participants

Throughout her research process, Dr Samira prioritised ethical considerations, ensuring that participants understood the purpose of her study and provided informed consent.

Maintaining anonymity and confidentiality was crucial; she protected participants' identities while reporting her findings. Additionally, she implemented measures to minimise harm, safeguarding participants from potential risks associated with discussing sensitive topics. Dr Samira remained mindful of community sensitivity, considering the broader impact of her research on the groups involved.

Summary: A Holistic Understanding of Experiences

After months of data collection and analysis, Dr Samira synthesised her findings, illustrating the multifaceted realities faced by individuals living with chronic illness. Her research showcased the complex interplay of personal, social, and institutional factors that shape their experiences. By employing a range of qualitative data collection techniques, Dr Samira captured the nuances of her participants' lives and ensured that their voices were represented.

In her presentation to colleagues at Willowbrook University, Dr Samira explained how qualitative research within the post-positivist framework allowed her to gain contextualised insights into the challenges faced by those with chronic illness. She highlighted the importance of understanding participants' perspectives and the limitations of relying solely on quantitative measures, which could overlook the complexity of human experiences.

Dr Samira's research highlighted the value of rigorous qualitative methods and their ability to uncover the complexities of social phenomena. She advocated for integrating qualitative approaches in research to foster a deeper understanding of human experiences.

Dr Samira's work exemplified how qualitative data collection techniques could yield profound insights, reflecting the lived experiences of individuals and enriching the understanding of complex social realities. Her approach demonstrated that embracing a diverse array of methodologies—while maintaining ethical integrity—could significantly enhance the impact of research within the post-positivist framework.

Conclusion

Qualitative data collection methods provide essential insights into human experiences. Researchers can contribute to a deeper understanding of complex social phenomena within the post-positivist framework by thoughtfully selecting methods and prioritising ethical considerations.

Table 11: Data Collection Techniques in Qualitative Research

Technique	Description	Strengths	Limitations
Interviews	Gather qualitative data through semi / structured and unstructured conversations.	Allows in-depth exploration of individual perspectives.	Structured interviews may limit depth; unstructured ones can lead to inconsistencies.
Focus Groups	Small groups discuss a specific topic, facilitating dynamic conversations and insights.	Reveals diverse perspectives and shared beliefs.	Group dynamics can hinder participation; dominant voices may overshadow others.
Observation	Systematic observation and documentation of behaviour in natural settings.	Provides real-world insights into social dynamics.	Risk of researcher influence; non-participant observation may limit depth.
Document Analysis	Examines existing documents to extract information related to research questions.	Offers insights into historical contexts and societal trends.	Documents may be biased or lack comprehensiveness.
Mixed Methods	Combines multiple qualitative techniques (and sometimes quantitative) for a comprehensive approach.	Enhances validity through triangulation of data.	Complexity in integrating methods and interpreting diverse data.

QUALITATIVE DATA ANALYSIS STRATEGIES IN THE POST-POSITIVIST FRAMEWORK

The next critical step is data analysis after gathering qualitative data through interviews, focus groups, observations, or document analysis. This phase involves organising and interpreting the rich information collected to uncover patterns and meanings. Unlike quantitative analysis, qualitative analysis is iterative and interpretive, making sense of complex social phenomena (Dawadi et al., 2021).

Key Analysis Strategies

<u>1. Thematic Analysis</u>

Thematic analysis identifies and reports patterns (themes) within the data (Buetow, 2025).

Process: Researchers immerse themselves in the data, read transcripts or notes, and identify initial codes (tags related to important information). They then group these codes into broader themes (Buetow, 2025). **Example**: In studying teachers' experiences during lockdown, a researcher could identify themes such as "adaptation to technology" and "emotional challenges."

Strengths: Flexible and widely applicable across various contexts.

Limitations: The risk of researcher bias during coding and theme development requires careful reflexivity (self-awareness of biases).

2. Narrative Analysis

Narrative analysis focuses on the stories people tell about their experiences (Delmas & Giles, 2022).

Process: Researchers examine the structure and content of narratives to understand meaning (Delmas & Giles, 2022).

Example: A study on addiction recovery could analyse personal stories, looking at common themes about coping strategies and support systems.

Strengths: Provides depth and insights into individual experiences.

Limitations: Requires careful interpretation to avoid imposing the researcher's perspective on the narratives.

3. Discourse Analysis

Discourse analysis examines language use in social contexts to understand how meaning is constructed (Delmas & Giles, 2022).

Process: Researchers analyse conversations, texts, or media, looking at word choice and context (Delmas & Giles, 2022). **Example**: Analysing media coverage on immigration may reveal how language reflects and shapes public opinions and stereotypes.

Strengths: Offers insights into power dynamics and social constructs.

Limitations: Requires a firm theoretical grounding and can be time-consuming.

Table 12: Qualitative Data Analysis Strategies in the Post-positivist Framework

Strategy	Description	Strengths	Limitations
Thematic Analysis	Identifies and reports patterns (themes) within the data.	Flexible and widely applicable	Risk of researcher bias in coding requires reflexivity.
Narrative Analysis	Focuses on the stories people tell to convey meaning.	Provides depth and insights into individual experiences.	Requires careful interpretation to avoid biases.
Discourse Analysis	Examines language use in social contexts to understand meaning construction.	Offers insights into power dynamics and social constructs.	Needs strong theoretical grounding; it can be time-consuming.

Data Collection Techniques

Qualitative data collection methods are diverse:

Interviews: These can be structured (set questions) or unstructured (more open-ended) to explore participants' thoughts. **Example**: An unstructured interview could ask, "What does social media mean to you?" allowing respondents to provide in-depth responses.

Focus Groups: Group discussions can reveal shared views and differing perspectives on a topic. **Example**: A focus group discussing a new community health initiative can illuminate varying opinions among participants.

Observational Studies: This involves systematically watching and documenting behaviour in natural settings. **Example**: A researcher may observe interactions in a community centre to understand how people seek support.

Table 13: Data Collection Techniques

Technique	Description	Example
Interviews	Collects qualitative data through set or open-ended questions.	An unstructured interview asking, "What does social media mean to you?"
Focus Groups	Group discussions that reveal shared and diverse perspectives.	Discussing community health initiatives to gather different opinions.
Observational Studies	Systematic observation of behaviour in natural settings.	Observing interactions at a community centre to understand support-seeking behaviours.

Rigorous Analysis and Ethical Considerations

The analysis process is essential and involves:

Coding: Identifying key themes from collected data.

Triangulation: Using multiple methods or data sources to confirm findings and enhance credibility.

Researchers should also be mindful of ethical considerations throughout the research process, including:

Informed Consent: Participants should know the study's purpose and agree to participate.

Confidentiality: Protecting participants' identities and data is paramount.

Hypothetically Unveiling Insights; Qualitative Data Analysis in Practice

At Eastfield College, Dr Olivia initiated a project to explore the experiences of individuals participating in community support programmes. After collecting qualitative data through interviews and focus groups, she moved to the critical data analysis step.

Understanding that this phase involved interpreting the information gathered, Dr Olivia aimed to uncover patterns and meanings within the data.

The Iterative Process of Qualitative Analysis

Dr Olivia recognised that qualitative analysis is iterative and interpretive, seeking to make sense of complex social phenomena while responding to the nuances of participants' lived experiences. She carefully selected strategies that aligned with her research goals.

1. Thematic Analysis: Identifying Patterns

Dr Olivia began with thematic analysis, which helped her identify and report patterns, or themes, within her data. She immersed herself in the interview transcripts and field notes, reading them thoroughly to become familiar with the content. As she did this, she identified initial codes—tags related to vital information that captured her participants' experiences.

For example, in studying teachers' experiences adapting to online instruction during lockdown, she identified themes such as "adaptation to technology" and "emotional challenges." This thematic identification provided a structured approach to understanding the broader implications of her findings.

Dr Olivia was aware of the risk of researcher bias during coding and theme development, which emphasised the need for reflexivity —maintaining self-awareness of her biases throughout the analysis process.

2. Narrative Analysis: Understanding Personal Stories

Dr Olivia also employed narrative analysis, focusing on individuals' stories about their experiences. In her study on community support, she examined personal narratives shared by participants about their journeys in seeking help. By analysing the structure and content of these narratives, Dr Olivia sought to uncover common themes related to coping mechanisms and support systems.

While narrative analysis offered valuable insights into individuals' experiences, Dr Olivia understood that careful interpretation was required to avoid imposing her perspective on participants' stories.

3. Discourse Analysis: Examining Language Use

Additionally, Dr Olivia incorporated discourse analysis, which examines language use in social contexts to understand how meaning is constructed. This method involved analysing conversations, texts, and other forms of communication to uncover how language shapes public opinion and social constructs. For instance, she conducted a discourse analysis of social media discussions surrounding community health initiatives, noting how language choices reflected and influenced public attitudes. This approach provided insights into the power dynamics at play within the community.

Despite the advantages of discourse analysis, Dr Olivia recognised that it required a solid theoretical grounding and could be time-consuming. She committed to furthering her understanding of the theoretical frameworks supporting her analysis.

Data Collection Techniques: A Diverse Approach

Throughout her research, Dr Olivia employed a range of data collection techniques, each tailored to her research questions.

Interviews: She conducted both structured and unstructured interviews to gather qualitative data. For instance, an unstructured interview could ask participants, "What does community support mean to you?" allowing them to express their thoughts in detail.

Focus Groups: Recognising the value of group dynamics, Dr Olivia organised focus groups to facilitate discussions among participants. A focus group discussing a new community health initiative could illuminate differing opinions and experiences, enhancing her understanding of community perceptions.

Observational Studies: Dr Olivia conducted observational studies to gain insights and systematically observe behaviours in natural settings. By observing activities in community centres, she aimed to understand how individuals sought support and engaged with one another.

Rigorous Analysis and Ethical Considerations

The analysis process involved several steps. Dr Olivia engaged in coding to identify key themes from the collected data, ensuring meticulous documentation of her analytical process. She also applied triangulation, using multiple methods and data sources to validate her findings.

Throughout her research journey, Dr Olivia prioritised ethical considerations. She obtained informed consent from all participants, ensuring they understood the study's purpose and willingly agreed to participate. Protecting participants' identities and data integrity was essential; she took measures to maintain confidentiality.

Summary: Contributing to Understanding Through Qualitative Analysis

After thorough analysis, Dr Olivia presented her findings, revealing the diverse experiences of individuals seeking community support. Her research highlighted the importance of combining various qualitative data analysis strategies, showcasing the complexity of human experiences.

In her presentation to colleagues at Eastfield College, Dr Olivia discussed how her use of thematic, narrative, and discourse analysis provided a multifaceted understanding of participants' perspectives. She highlighted the significance of capturing the intricacies of human behaviour and the insights that qualitative research can contribute to social science.

Dr Olivia's work demonstrated that qualitative data analysis involves deep engagement with the data and focusing on participants' experiences. This allowed her to shed light on the dynamics of community support, informing practices and interventions designed to enhance wellbeing.

Conclusion

Qualitative data analysis within the post-positivist framework is essential for understanding complex social phenomena. Through strategies like thematic analysis, narrative analysis, and discourse analysis, researchers gain valuable insights into human experiences.

By thoughtfully applying these methods and maintaining a commitment to transparency and reflexivity, researchers can contribute meaningfully to understanding social issues, advancing knowledge responsibly within the post-positivist paradigm. Effective qualitative research embodies both rigour and sensitivity, preparing researchers to navigate the complexities of human experience.

UNDERSTANDING CREDIBILITY AND TRANSFERABILITY IN QUALITATIVE RESEARCH

After discussing qualitative data analysis techniques, we now focus on the crucial aspects of credibility and transferability, which are key to assessing the trustworthiness of qualitative research. In contrast to quantitative research, which relies on statistical measures, qualitative research employs specific criteria to ensure its rigour (Korstjens & Moser, 2017).

Credibility

Credibility refers to the confidence researchers can have in the truthfulness of their findings. It reflects how accurately the research captures participants' perspectives and experiences. To establish credibility, researchers should (Korstjens & Moser, 2017):

Engage Deeply: Spend ample time in the research setting to build rapport with participants, gaining a richer understanding. For instance, if studying community health beliefs, immersing oneself in the community can lead to deeper insights.

Use Triangulation: This involves incorporating multiple data sources or methods to verify findings. For example, combining interviews with surveys and document analysis helps ensure a well-rounded perspective.

Member Checking: In this process, researchers share their interpretations with participants, ensuring that the study reflects their lived experiences.

This feedback enhances the accuracy of the findings.

Reflexivity: Researchers should know their biases and how they could influence their interpretations. Acknowledging personal perspectives strengthens the credibility of the research.

Crystallisation: This approach extends triangulation by considering different aspects or viewpoints to form a more comprehensive understanding of the phenomenon. It involves examining the same data from multiple angles, enriching interpretations. For example, reflecting on a participant's story from psychological, cultural, and social perspectives can lead to deeper insights (Keyter & Roos, 2015).

Transferability

Transferability relates to how findings can be applied to other contexts or populations. Rather than seeking broad generalisability, qualitative research provides detailed descriptions of the research context. This rich context enables readers to assess whether the findings may be relevant in their own situations (Roos et al., 2016).

Example: In a study of educational interventions, a detailed account of the school environment, the student demographic, and the teaching methods allows others in similar settings to evaluate the applicability of the findings to their own context.

Dependability

Dependability is about the consistency of the research findings over time and across different researchers. Researchers can enhance dependability by systematically documenting their research process, including the decisions and actions taken throughout the study. This transparency allows others to follow their reasoning.

Inter-Rater Reliability: Involving multiple researchers in data collection and analysis can also improve dependability by minimising individual bias. If different researchers arrive at similar conclusions, this increases confidence in the findings.

Confirmability

Confirmability pertains to the neutrality of the research findings, ensuring they reflect the data rather than the researchers' biases.

Researchers can enhance confirmability by keeping detailed records of their research process and the rationale for their decisions. This allows others to review the connections between the data and the conclusions drawn.

By using **crystallisation**, researchers look at the data from various perspectives. This multi-faceted approach strengthens confirmability by providing a fuller picture of the studied phenomenon. For example, examining a participant's experience through different lenses—such as psychological, social, and cultural—can reveal multiple interpretations and insights. This not only enriches understanding but also helps ensure that findings are robust and reflective of diverse experiences.

Triangulation similarly contributes to confirmability by incorporating multiple sources or methods to corroborate findings, thereby reinforcing the credibility of the results.

Hypothetical example on how to Ensure Trustworthiness: Credibility and Transferability in Qualitative Research

At Greenfield University, Dr Rachel initiated a project to understand the experiences of first-generation university students. Recognising the importance of credibility and transferability in her research, she focused on assessing the trustworthiness of her qualitative findings while navigating the complexities of human experiences.

Credibility: Establishing Confidence in Findings

Dr Rachel understood that credibility refers to confidence in her findings' truthfulness. It reflects how accurately her research captures the perspectives and experiences of her participants. To establish credibility, she employed several strategies:

Engaging Deeply: Dr Rachel spent time in the university setting, attending events and engaging with first-generation students. She built rapport with participants by immersing herself in the community, leading to more substantial insights into their experiences.

Using Triangulation: Dr Rachel incorporated multiple data sources and methods to verify her findings. She combined interviews with focus groups and document analysis of student support materials. This multifaceted approach ensured a comprehensive perspective on the challenges and successes faced by first-generation students.

Member Checking: To enhance the accuracy of her interpretations, Dr Rachel shared her findings with participants and sought their feedback. This process confirmed that her study aligned with their lived experiences and allowed participants to offer additional insights.

Reflexivity: Throughout her research, Dr Rachel maintained a reflexive stance, continuously reflecting on her own biases and how they may influence her interpretations. By acknowledging her perspectives, she strengthened the credibility of her research process.

Crystallisation: Dr Rachel employed the concept of crystallisation, which extends the idea of triangulation. By considering different aspects and viewpoints, she examined the same data from various angles, enriching her interpretations. For instance, she reflected on a participant's journey from psychological, social, and cultural perspectives to achieve a deeper understanding of their experiences.

Transferability: Applying Findings to Other Contexts

As Dr Rachel articulated her findings, she embraced the concept of transferability—the extent to which her results could be applied to other contexts or populations. Instead of seeking broad generalisability, she provided detailed descriptions of her research context.

For example, she offered a thorough account of the university environment, including the demographic makeup of the student body and the specific challenges first-generation students face. This detailed presentation enabled readers in similar settings to evaluate the relevance of her findings to their contexts.

Dependability: Ensuring Consistency in Findings

Dr Rachel recognised that dependability pertained to the consistency of her findings over time and across different researchers. To enhance dependability, she systematically documented her research process, noting the decisions and actions taken throughout the study. This transparency allowed others to follow her reasoning and understand the context of her conclusions.

Involving multiple researchers in data collection and analysis also contributed to dependability. By engaging colleagues in her study, they collectively analysed the data, increasing confidence in the findings if different researchers arrived at similar conclusions.

Confirmability: Ensuring Neutrality in Findings

Dr Rachel emphasised confirmability, ensuring that her findings accurately reflected the data rather than any preconceived biases she may have held. She maintained detailed records of her research process to achieve this, documenting the rationale behind her decisions. This allowed others to review the connections she made between the data and her conclusions.

By employing crystallisation, Dr Rachel examined the data from multiple perspectives. This multifaceted approach strengthened confirmability, providing a fuller view of the phenomenon being studied. For example, analysing a participant's experience of transitioning to university through various lenses revealed multiple interpretations and insights.

Additionally, Dr Rachel used triangulation within the data collection, incorporating various sources and methods to corroborate her findings, reinforcing the credibility of her results and their confirmability.

Summary: Upholding Rigour in Qualitative Research

After completing her research and analysing the data, Dr Rachel presented her findings to her colleagues at Greenfield University. She emphasised the importance of acknowledging and addressing the limitations inherent in qualitative research. While she had achieved robust evidence for the examined relationships, she recognised challenges such as striving for complete objectivity, ensuring valid generalisations, and managing potential biases.

From her experiences, Dr Rachel outlined strategies for enhancing the quality of qualitative research: rigorous research design, careful data collection, and critical self-awareness of biases. She encouraged her peers to integrate various research methods and maintain transparency in their studies.

Ultimately, Dr Rachel's work illustrated that a balanced approach, recognising both the strengths and limitations of qualitative research, is essential for advancing social science research. By acknowledging these challenges, researchers could contribute valuable insights to understanding complex social phenomena.

Conclusion

In summary, establishing credibility, transferability, dependability, and confirmability is essential for the rigour and impact of qualitative research. These criteria are akin to validity and reliability in quantitative research but are tailored to the interpretive nature of qualitative inquiry.

Researchers can enhance the quality and trustworthiness of their findings by employing strategies such as prolonged engagement, triangulation, member checking, reflexivity, and crystallisation. Crystallisation allows for multiple perspectives on the data, enriching interpretations and ensuring that findings reflect the complexity of human experiences.

A transparent approach bolsters qualitative research's integrity and facilitates critical engagement and replication by other researchers. Ultimately, the goal is to contribute meaningfully to our understanding of social phenomena through well-conducted qualitative research using diverse methods that capture the richness of the human experience.

MIXED METHODS RESEARCH: BRIDGING THE POSITIVIST-POST-POSITIVIST DIVIDE

I n our exploration of qualitative research, we recognised the importance of integrating approaches to understand complex social phenomena comprehensively. Mixed methods research combines quantitative and qualitative techniques within a single study, providing a powerful way to bridge the divide between positivist and post-positivist frameworks (Busetto et al., 2020).

This approach is not just about adding quantitative and qualitative methods together; it's about leveraging the strengths of both to address the limitations inherent in each. For instance, quantitative methods effectively measure and identify patterns across large datasets, while qualitative methods delve into the richness of human experiences, providing context and depth (Dawadi et al., 2021).

Applications of Mixed Methods

Explanatory Sequential Design: In this approach, quantitative data is collected first, followed by qualitative data to explain the findings (Edmonds & Kennedy, 2017). For example, a researcher may conduct a survey measuring public health behaviours and then hold interviews with participants to explore their motivations for these behaviours.

Exploratory Sequential Design: Here, qualitative data is collected first to generate hypotheses, which are then tested using quantitative methods (Shiyanbola et al., 2021). For example, researchers could interview students about their challenges with online learning and subsequently develop a survey to quantify those challenges across a larger population.

Concurrent Design: This involves collecting both quantitative and qualitative data simultaneously (Bell, Warren, & Schmidt, 2022).

For instance, a researcher may administer a survey on attitudes towards climate change while conducting focus groups to understand the reasons behind those attitudes. The simultaneous collection allows for more integrated findings.

Key Considerations for Mixed Methods Research

Research Question: The research question should clearly justify using mixed methods. It should explain how both data types will complement each other to address different aspects of the problem.

Method Selection: Choose appropriate quantitative and qualitative methods to suit the research question. Both should align with the study's objectives and ensure data compatibility. For example, if a specific statistical test is used in the quantitative phase, the qualitative method should enhance understanding of the same phenomenon.

Data Integration Strategy: Researchers should clearly document how they will integrate the two data types. This could involve comparing the findings of the survey and focus groups to provide a fuller picture of public opinion on climate change.

Ethical Considerations: It is crucial to maintain ethical standards throughout the research. This includes obtaining informed consent, ensuring confidentiality, and treating all data respectfully, especially when integrating findings from diverse sources.

Reporting Findings: The report should thoroughly describe the research design, methodology, and how the two data components were integrated. This transparency helps ensure the credibility and reproducibility of the research.

Table 14: Continuum of Research Paradigms: Positivist to Post-positivist

Paradigm	Focus of Inquiry	Key Features	Types of Data
Positivist	Objective measurement	- Emphasis on quantifiable data - Use of randomised controlled trials - Statistical analysis - Aim for generalisability	Primarily quantitative
Mixed Methods	Integration of both paradigms	- Combines quantitative and qualitative methods - Leverages strengths of both approaches	Both quantitative and qualitative
Post-positivist	Subjective understanding	- Emphasis on contextual and lived experiences - Use of narrative perspectives - Focus on rich descriptions	Primarily qualitative

Interpretation

The table illustrates the transition from positivist to post-positivist paradigms. Positivism focuses on objective measurement and quantifiable data, while post-positivism embraces the complexities of human experience through qualitative methods. Mixed methods serve as a bridge, integrating both approaches for a well-rounded perspective.

Example on how to Bridge the Divide: Mixed Methods Research at Harmony University

At Harmony University, Dr Alex recognised the limitations of relying solely on quantitative or qualitative methods when examining complex social phenomena. To gain a comprehensive understanding of the challenges faced by students during their transition to university life, he adopted a mixed methods research approach. This methodology provided a framework for integrating both quantitative and qualitative techniques within a single study.

The Rationale Behind Mixed Methods Research

Dr Alex understood that mixed methods research involves leveraging the strengths of both approaches to address their inherent limitations. Quantitative methods facilitate measuring and identifying patterns across large datasets, while qualitative methods provide depth and context by exploring human experiences.

<u>Applications of Mixed Methods</u>

To implement his research effectively, Dr Alex outlined a clear explanatory sequential design. He planned to collect quantitative data first, followed by qualitative data to contextualise the findings. For instance, he designed a survey measuring students' stress and anxiety levels related to their university experience. After collecting the survey data, he interviewed selected participants to explore their motivations and experiences surrounding their stress.

In addition, Dr Alex considered an exploratory sequential design, whereby he would gather qualitative data first to generate hypotheses, which he would test using quantitative methods. For example, he could conduct focus group discussions with students to identify common challenges faced during their transition to university life. Based on these discussions, he would develop a survey to quantify the prevalence of these challenges across a larger student population.

Another option in his research toolkit was the concurrent design, where quantitative and qualitative data would be collected simultaneously. For instance, while administering a survey on student satisfaction with university services, he could engage in focus groups to understand the reasons behind varying satisfaction levels. This simultaneous collection would provide a more integrated understanding of student experiences.

<u>Key Considerations for Mixed Methods Research</u>

As Dr Alex developed his mixed methods framework, he recognised several key considerations vital for the success of his research:

Research Question: He ensured that his research question justified the use of mixed methods, articulating how both data types would complement each other in addressing different aspects of the issue.

Method Selection: Dr Alex selected appropriate quantitative and qualitative methods aligned with his research objectives. For instance, if a specific statistical test was used in the quantitative phase, the qualitative method chosen would enhance understanding of the same phenomena.

Data Integration Strategy: A clear plan for integrating quantitative and qualitative data was crucial. Dr Alex documented how he would compare the survey and focus group findings to provide a fuller picture of student experiences and satisfaction.

Ethical Considerations: High ethical standards were maintained throughout the research process. Dr Alex focused on obtaining informed consent, ensuring confidentiality, and treating all data respectfully as he integrated findings from diverse sources.

Reporting Findings: Dr Alex recognised the importance of thoroughly describing his research design and methodology when sharing his results. Transparency regarding how the two data components were integrated would enhance the credibility and reproducibility of his research.

<u>Conclusion: A Comprehensive Perspective on Student Experiences</u>

After completing his data collection and analysis, Dr Alex presented his findings, revealing an understanding of students' challenges and successes during their transition to university. By employing mixed methods research, he bridged the divide between positivist and post-positivist frameworks, combining the strengths of both approaches to provide a comprehensive perspective.

His research provided insights into the academic community and offered recommendations for university administrators seeking to improve student support services. By demonstrating the value of mixed methods, Dr Alex encouraged colleagues at Harmony University to consider this integrative approach in their own research, facilitating discussions about the complexities of human experience in educational settings.

In conclusion, mixed methods research offers a robust approach to understanding complex social issues by combining the strengths of quantitative and qualitative methods. By thoughtfully considering research design, data collection, integration strategies, and ethical guidelines, researchers can yield richer insights than would be possible with either approach alone. This methodology represents a significant advancement in social science research, allowing for deeper exploration that bridges the positivist-post-positivist divide.

Conclusion

In conclusion, mixed methods research offers a robust approach to understanding complex social issues by combining the strengths of quantitative and qualitative methods. By thoughtfully considering research design, data collection, integration strategies, and ethical guidelines, researchers can yield richer insights than would be possible with either approach alone.

This methodology represents a significant advancement in social science research, allowing for deeper exploration that bridges the positivist-post-positivist divide. With careful planning and methodological rigour, researchers can navigate the intricacies of mixed methods to produce impactful findings that contribute meaningfully to our understanding of the social world.

CHAPTER 4: CONSTRUCTIVISM AND CRITICAL REALISM WITHIN POST-POSITIVISM

CONSTRUCTIVISM: THE SOCIAL CONSTRUCTION OF REALITY

Constructivism, a key perspective within post-positivism, challenges the idea of an objective reality that exists independently of the observer (Denicolo, Long, & Bradley-Cole, 2016). Instead, it posits that reality is socially constructed through interaction and shared meaning-making processes. This means we actively create knowledge through our experiences and social contexts rather than passively receiving it (Shannon-Baker, 2023). This perspective aligns closely with critical realism, which acknowledges the existence of real-world structures that influence our understanding while emphasising that social contexts shape our interpretations.

Key Concepts in Constructivism

Meaning-Making: The core tenet of constructivism is that meaning is created through social engagement (Shannon-Baker, 2023). For instance, the concept of "family" varies across cultures; in some communities, family includes extended relatives, while in others, it may solely refer to parents and children. This illustrates how cultural beliefs and practices shape meanings, highlighting the interplay between social realities and individual perceptions.

Subjectivity: Constructivists recognise that researchers are part of the social world they study. Their perspectives, biases, and experiences shape their interpretations. This doesn't invalidate research; instead, it highlights the need for reflexivity—researchers should reflect on how their backgrounds influence their work (Shannon-Baker, 2023).

Qualitative Approaches Suitable for Constructivism

Qualitative research methods align with constructivism, allowing for in-depth exploration of human experiences (Shannon-Baker, 2023).

Ethnography: This method involves immersing oneself in a culture to observe and understand social practices (Denicolo et al., 2016). For instance, an ethnographer could live in a community to study local health beliefs, gaining rich insights from participants.

Grounded Theory: This approach starts by collecting data and building theories from the ground up (Denicolo et al., 2016). For example, interviewing cancer patients about their experiences can reveal new insights into coping mechanisms, generating theories about resilience, reflecting the dynamic interplay between individual agency and social conditions.

Case Studies: Investigating a specific case, like a school implementing a new curriculum, provides an in-depth understanding of factors influencing success. Researchers gather data from various sources, including interviews and documents, to paint a comprehensive picture (Denicolo et al., 2016), acknowledging how context shapes outcomes.

Data Analysis Techniques

Qualitative data analysis is iterative, involving several stages:

Familiarisation: Researchers immerse themselves in the data to grasp its overall meaning, understanding how personal and contextual factors inform interpretations.

Coding: Identifying key themes and patterns in the data helps clarify meanings. For example, coding interviews with adolescents about social media use may uncover themes related to self-image and peer pressure, illustrating how social influences affect individual experiences.

Thematic Analysis: This method looks for recurring themes, providing insights into everyday experiences among participants and thereby illuminating the complexities of social realities.

Evaluating Trustworthiness

To ensure credibility and trustworthiness in qualitative research, researchers focus on:

Credibility: Building confidence in the findings through triangulation (using multiple methods or data sources) and member checking (involving participants in reviewing interpretations).

Transferability: Providing contextual details enables readers to determine the applicability of findings to their own settings, reflecting the importance of situating understanding within broader frameworks.

Dependability: Maintaining consistency in research processes through detailed documentation enhances reliability through evolving social contexts.

Confirmability: Ensuring findings reflect the data, not the researchers' biases, can be achieved through transparent processes and reflexivity, which align with the principles of critical realism and constructivism.

Constructing Reality; Hypnotical Exploration Constructivism at Meadowbrook University

At Meadowbrook University, Dr Emma initiated a research project to understand how individuals make sense of their experiences in the context of mental health support. Adopting constructivism as a key perspective within the post-positivist framework, she sought to challenge the notion of an objective reality that exists independently of the observer. Dr Emma proposed that knowledge construction is fundamentally social, with interaction and shared meaning shaping reality.

Understanding Key Concepts in Constructivism

Dr Emma identified meaning-making as the core principle of constructivism. She recognised that the meanings individuals ascribe to concepts are constructed through social engagement and cultural contexts. For example, the definition of "community" can vary significantly across cultures, affecting individuals' experiences and perceptions.

In her research, Dr Emma acknowledged the importance of subjectivity. As a constructivist, she understood her own perspectives, biases, and experiences would influence her interpretations. By emphasising reflexivity, she reflected on how her background shaped her research, ensuring she maintained awareness of her influence on the study.

Qualitative Approaches Aligned with Constructivism

Given the nature of her inquiry, Dr Emma opted for qualitative research methods that aligned with the constructivist approach, enabling an in-depth exploration of human experiences.

Ethnography: Dr Emma immersed herself in the community where her study participants resided. By engaging with individuals in their daily environments, she aimed to observe and understand social practices surrounding mental health support, gathering comprehensive qualitative data.

Grounded Theory: Recognising that existing theories may not adequately capture her findings, she employed grounded theory. Dr Emma began conducting interviews with individuals about their experiences with mental health support, allowing for the development of theories based on the data collected. This approach aimed to reveal insights into coping mechanisms and resilience among participants.

Case Studies: Dr Emma conducted case studies of specific community mental health initiatives. For example, she examined a programme designed to support individuals with anxiety, gathering data from interviews with participants, programme facilitators, and related documents. This focused approach facilitated a detailed understanding of factors influencing the programme's effectiveness.

Data Analysis Techniques: An Iterative Process

Dr Emma understood that qualitative data analysis is inherently iterative, involving multiple stages:

Familiarisation: She immersed herself in the collected data, reviewing transcripts to discern the overall meaning and context of participants' experiences.

Coding: Dr Emma engaged in coding to identify key themes and patterns within the data. For example, coding interviews regarding mental health support could uncover recurring themes such as feelings of isolation and the importance of peer relationships.

Thematic Analysis: Using thematic analysis, Dr Emma examined recurrent themes throughout her data, providing insights into shared everyday experiences among her participants.

Evaluating Trustworthiness: Building Credibility

To ensure the trustworthiness of her qualitative research, Dr Emma focused on several essential aspects:

Credibility: She aimed to enhance confidence in her findings through triangulation, using multiple methods and data sources to corroborate her results. Additionally, she incorporated member checking, inviting participants to review her interpretations to ensure an accurate reflection of their experiences.

Transferability: Dr Emma provided contextual details within her study, enabling readers to assess the applicability of her findings to their own contexts, thereby enhancing transferability.

Dependability: Dr Emma maintained comprehensive documentation of her methodology and decision-making throughout the research process. This transparency allowed others to understand the context of her conclusions and enhanced the dependability of her findings.

Confirmability: Dr Emma focused on maintaining an objective stance to ensure her findings accurately reflected the data. She kept detailed records of her data analysis and engaged in reflexive practices to address potential biases, ensuring her conclusions were grounded in the data collected.

<u>Conclusion: Constructing Understanding Through Qualitative Research</u>

After completing her research and data analysis, Dr Emma presented her findings, revealing the complexities faced by individuals navigating mental health support. Her commitment to constructivist principles within the post-positivist framework illustrated the effectiveness of qualitative research in providing insights into human experiences.

In her presentation at Meadowbrook University, Dr Emma explained how using qualitative research methods allowed her to explore meaning-making processes in depth. By integrating various qualitative methods and grounding her work in principles of credibility, transferability, dependability, and confirmability, she provided a nuanced understanding of participants' lived experiences.

Dr Emma's research highlighted the significance of qualitative methods within the post-positivist framework. Her findings contributed insights to the academic community and offered practical implications for policymakers and practitioners in mental health support.

In conclusion, Dr Emma's exploration of constructivism emphasized the value of qualitative research in uncovering the complexities of social realities. By employing robust data analysis strategies and maintaining ethical considerations, she demonstrated that qualitative inquiry is essential for understanding human experiences comprehensively.

Conclusion

In conclusion, constructivism offers a valuable framework for understanding how human interactions shape social reality. By acknowledging the active role of individuals in meaning-making, constructivism helps to explore the complexities of social phenomena. However, addressing its limitations—particularly the risk of relativism—requires rigorous methodology, transparency, and critical reflection.

The strength of constructivism lies in its ability to uncover the rich tapestry of meanings that define our social world. By balancing in-depth exploration of specific contexts with the quest for generalisable insights, researchers can contribute significantly to understanding human experiences.

CRITICAL REALISM: ACKNOWLEDGING UNDERLYING STRUCTURES

Critical realism presents a nuanced approach within the post-positivist framework based on the constructivist perspective that reality is socially constructed (Fletcher, 2017). Unlike constructivism, which focuses on subjective interpretations, critical realism asserts that an objective reality exists independently, though social structures and processes often obscure it (Shannon-Baker, 2023).

Key Concepts in Critical Realism

Critical realism provides a framework to understand reality through three domains:

Three Domains of Reality:

Empirical: This domain includes observable phenomena—what can be seen and measured, such as survey responses or participant behaviours (Fletcher, 2017).

Actual: This refers to events and processes that occur, whether or not they are observed. It highlights that reality encompasses happenings that may go unnoticed by researchers (Fletcher, 2017).

Real: The real domain includes underlying structures and mechanisms that generate both actual and empirical outcomes. Often hidden, these factors encompass sociocultural, economic, and political influences that shape experiences(Fletcher, 2017).

Example: In studying unemployment rates, the empirical data could show how many people are unemployed, while the actual factors could include factory closures and economic conditions. The real influences could be broader societal structures, like economic policies and historical development.

Understanding Social Phenomena: Critical realism encourages researchers to look beyond observable events to understand the deeper forces at play. This approach recognises the complexity of social interactions and challenges simplistic cause-and-effect relationships (Shannon-Baker, 2023).

Research Methodologies in Critical Realism

Critical realist research often uses various methodologies to understand the interplay between structures and individual actions (Dawadi et al., 2021).

Mixed Methods: Combining quantitative data (e.g., statistical analysis) with qualitative insights (e.g., interviews) enriches the research findings (Fletcher, 2017). For instance, when researching educational inequality, a researcher could start with statistics on student performance and follow up with interviews to understand the personal experiences underlying those numbers.

Identifying Mechanisms: A critical realist approach looks for the mechanisms linking the real, actual, and empirical domains (Fletcher, 2017). In the context of educational outcomes, researchers could investigate how funding disparities between schools directly affect student performance, thereby linking structural factors to observed achievements.

Challenges of Critical Realism

Despite its strengths, critical realism faces some challenges (Shannon-Baker, 2023):

Interpretative Flexibility: Different researchers may interpret the same data in various ways, potentially leading to different conclusions. This variability underscores the need for methodological rigour and transparency (Fletcher, 2017).

Complexity and Resources: The multi-layered nature of critical realist research can be time-consuming and resource-intensive. Successfully integrating various methodologies requires careful planning and sufficient expertise (Shannon-Baker, 2023).

Uncovering Realities: Hypothetical Journey into Critical Realism at Crestwood College

At Crestwood College, Dr Benjamin initiated a project to understand the complexities of educational inequality. While incorporating the constructivist perspective that reality is socially constructed, he recognised the value of critical realism as a framework for exploring the underlying structures that shape social phenomena.

Understanding Key Concepts in Critical Realism

Dr Benjamin embraced the concept that while subjective interpretations are significant, an objective reality exists independently of individual perceptions. He understood that social structures and processes influencing human behaviours and outcomes often obscure this reality.

One foundational idea explored by Dr Benjamin was the three domains of reality:

Empirical: This domain encompasses observable phenomena, including all that can be seen and measured. For instance, empirical data on educational inequality may reveal varying student performance scores across different schools.

Actual: This refers to events and processes that occur, even if they are not directly observed. For example, incidents of student dropout may not be recorded, but they still influence the educational landscape.

Real: This domain involves the underlying structures and mechanisms that generate the actual and empirical outcomes, often hidden from view. For instance, when examining unemployment rates, empirical data would indicate how many people are unemployed. At the same time, the real influences could encompass broader societal structures, such as economic policies and historical context.

Dr Benjamin aimed to demonstrate how critical realism encourages researchers to look beyond observable events to recognise the deeper forces, challenging simplistic cause-and-effect relationships by clearly distinguishing these domains.

Research Methodologies in Critical Realism

Dr Benjamin adopted a mixed methods approach to explore the interplay between structures and individual actions, combining both quantitative and qualitative methodologies in his research.

In studying educational inequality, he first collected quantitative data on student performance across various demographics and schools. This statistical analysis provided a foundation for understanding the scale of the issue, but Dr Benjamin recognised that quantitative data alone would not offer a complete picture.

He gathered qualitative insights through interviews with students, teachers, and parents to enrich his findings. For example, he asked participants about their experiences and perceptions regarding educational resources and support systems. This combination allowed him to contextualise the statistical data, revealing the lived realities behind the numbers.

Moreover, Dr Benjamin focused on identifying mechanisms that link the real, actual, and empirical domains. While exploring educational outcomes, he investigated how school funding disparities impacted student performance. By connecting different domains, he aimed to uncover the mechanisms influencing the educational experience and outcomes for students from diverse backgrounds.

Challenges of Critical Realism

Despite its advantages, Dr Benjamin faced several challenges while conducting critical realist research. One significant challenge was interpretive flexibility. With a diverse team of researchers analysing the same data, differing interpretations could arise, potentially leading to varying conclusions. This variability underscored the need for methodological rigour and transparency throughout the research process.

The complexity and resource demands of critical realist research also presented hurdles. The multi-layered nature of integrating various methodologies could be time-consuming and require careful planning. As Dr Benjamin developed his approach, he recognised the importance of assembling a skilled team and ensuring adequate resources to undertake such a comprehensive endeavour.

Conclusion: Unveiling Underlying Structures

After completing his research and analysis, Dr Benjamin presented his findings, revealing the underlying structures influencing educational inequality. His research documented statistical disparities in student performance and provided qualitative insights into the experiences of those impacted by these inequalities.

In his presentation at Crestwood College, Dr Benjamin explained how critical realism bridges surface observations and the underlying realities of social structures.

By employing mixed methods and focusing on the mechanisms linking different domains, he demonstrated the effectiveness of critical realism in exploring complex social phenomena.

Dr Benjamin's work underscored the potential of critical realism to enhance the understanding of educational and societal issues. By examining the interactions between structures and individual experiences, he encouraged fellow researchers to apply critical realist methodologies in their studies, fostering further exploration of the realities that shape the social world.

Conclusion

In conclusion, critical realism offers a valuable framework for exploring how underlying structures shape social phenomena. Acknowledging an objective reality while considering the limitations of human observation presents a sophisticated approach to social research.

Critical realism enhances our understanding by focusing on the mechanisms driving observable effects and integrating multiple methods to build a comprehensive picture. While it presents specific challenges, its depth of insight makes it a crucial tool for social scientists aiming to grasp the complexities of the social world. Committed researchers can navigate these challenges effectively, contributing to a richer understanding of social issues.

COMPARING CONSTRUCTIVISM AND CRITICAL REALISM

onstructivism and critical realism are both philosophical approaches to knowledge and reality. They are non-reductionists, sharing a belief in the existence of natural phenomena. However, they differ significantly in their views on the relationship between knowledge and the world and the role of social structures in causing events (Fodouop Kouam, 2024; Shannon-Baker, 2023).

Constructivism

Constructivism emphasises that reality is socially constructed through interactions and shared meanings. Knowledge is not a mere reflection of objective truth but is shaped by social experiences and context (Shannon-Baker, 2023).

Key Features

Subjectivity: Researchers actively participate in knowledge creation, influencing their interpretations. For example, a researcher observing family dynamics should recognise how their own background may affect their understanding of what family means in different cultures (Fodouop Kouam, 2024).

Multiple Interpretations: There are no single, universally valid interpretations. Different individuals can have equally valid views of the same event, such as how a community understands mental health (Fodouop Kouam, 2024).

Strengths

Captures the nuances of human experience and provides rich, contextual insights into social interactions.

Limitations

Generalisability can be tricky since findings may not apply to wider populations. For instance, a study on a small, specific group may not reflect the experiences of other communities. The lack of objective standards can make establishing the validity of findings challenging.

Critical Realism

In contrast, critical realism asserts that an objective reality exists, although social structures and human interpretation influence our understanding of it (Shannon-Baker, 2023).

Key Features

Underlying Structures: It posits that there are deeper mechanisms that create observable phenomena (Fodouop Kouam, 2024). For example, in studying unemployment rates, a critical realist would explore the statistics and the societal factors contributing to those rates, like economic policies or local job markets.

Retroduction: A process where researchers move from observed effects to identify the underlying causes (Shannon-Baker, 2023). For instance, while exploring educational outcomes, researchers may examine how funding disparities between schools directly impact student performance.

Strengths

Able to explain causal relationships by recognising the complexities behind social phenomena.

Limitations

The process of retroduction can be complex and difficult to apply, requiring rigorous analysis (Fodouop Kouam, 2024).

There's a risk of emphasising structural influences to the detriment of individual agency, meaning that the role of personal choice in shaping outcomes may be understated.

Complementary Use of Frameworks

When comparing constructivism and critical realism, choosing one over the other isn't simply about which one is better; each has unique strengths that suit different research questions (Shannon-Baker, 2023).

Constructivism: Ideal for exploring rich, subjective experiences, particularly in qualitative studies focused on meaning-making. Its emphasis on context-specific understanding makes it powerful for exploring the diverse ways people construct their realities (Fodouop Kouam, 2024).

Critical Realism: More appropriate for research aimed at uncovering causal mechanisms and developing theories that can be applied more broadly (Shannon-Baker, 2023). For instance, it effectively identifies the underlying social structures that influence health outcomes.

Often, researchers benefit from integrating elements from both frameworks. Researchers can cultivate a more holistic view of social realities by acknowledging individual experiences' richness and the need to understand the structures influencing those experiences.

Conclusion

Choosing between constructivism and critical realism depends on the research question and context. Both frameworks offer valuable insights and can be complementary in providing a deeper understanding of social phenomena.

Table 15: Comparison of Constructivism and Critical Realism

Aspect	Constructivism	Critical Realism
Core Idea	Reality is socially constructed through interactions and shared meanings.	An objective reality exists, though social structures and human interpretations often obscure it.
Subjectivity	Researchers actively shape knowledge based on their own perspectives.	Researchers acknowledge their influence but strive for objectivity in understanding the underlying structures.
Multiple Interpretations	Emphasises that multiple, equally valid interpretations of phenomena can coexist.	Recognises the importance of identifying causal mechanisms and acknowledges that understanding is influenced by context.
Research Focus	Explores personal experiences and meanings; e.g., studying how individuals define "family."	Investigates underlying structures; e.g., examining socioeconomic factors contributing to unemployment rates.
Strengths	Captures the richness and complexity of human experiences; reveals hidden power dynamics.	Explains causal relationships; integrates qualitative and quantitative data for a comprehensive analysis.
Limitations	Challenges with generalisability; subjective interpretations may lead to bias.	Complexity in applying retroduction; potential overemphasis on structures may downplay individual agency.
Ideal Methods	Qualitative techniques like ethnography, narrative analysis, and case studies to capture subjective experiences.	Mixed methods, including qualitative interviews and quantitative data analysis, to explore causal mechanisms.

Hypothetical Case Studies: Applying Constructivist and Critical Realist Approaches

T o illustrate the practical applications of constructivism and critical realism, let's delve into two case studies highlighting how these frameworks are employed in real research projects. By examining these examples, we can better understand their strengths and limitations and researchers' methodological choices based on their philosophical commitments.

1. Constructivist Study: Immigrant Women's Healthcare Experiences

In our first case study, a researcher decided to explore the experiences of immigrant women navigating the healthcare system in a new country. This topic is rich with complexity, as it intertwines cultural norms, personal experiences, and societal structures.

The researcher adopted a constructivist approach to understand how these women perceive their healthcare interactions. Instead of seeking objective measurements or universal truths, the researcher set out to uncover the diverse meanings these women attribute to their experiences. To do this, she organised in-depth interviews, allowing the women to share their stories openly.

During these interviews, the researcher created a safe space for participants to express their feelings about accessing healthcare services. She asked broad questions, encouraging the women to discuss their experiences with healthcare providers and the cultural differences and language barriers they faced. Through careful listening and probing follow-up questions, the researcher identified key themes that emerged, such as fear, confusion, and the importance of community support.

The researcher recognised that her own experience as an immigrant woman could shape the questions she asked and how she interpreted the responses. By being reflexive—reflecting critically on her own biases—she aimed to present the women's narratives authentically. The analysis of the interview data involved thematic analysis, where recurring patterns and themes were identified.

For instance, some women spoke of the stigma they felt when seeking help, while others highlighted how cultural misunderstandings affected their treatment. By compiling these rich narratives, the researcher built a detailed ethnographic account that revealed the multifaceted nature of healthcare access for immigrant women, showcasing the intricate interplay between identity, culture, and health.

2. Critical Realist Study: Social Media and Political Polarisation

In contrast, our second case study involves a researcher studying the impact of social media on political polarisation. This researcher approached the topic with a critical realist perspective, believing that while social media creates observable effects on political behaviour, these effects are driven by deeper underlying structures and mechanisms.

The researcher hypothesised that algorithmic filtering on social media platforms may contribute to the formation of echo chambers, where users are only exposed to viewpoints that reinforce their pre-existing beliefs. The researcher employed a mixed-methods design to investigate this, first gathering quantitative data on social media usage patterns and political attitudes through surveys.

Then, to delve deeper into the subjective experiences of social media users, the researcher conducted qualitative interviews. Participants shared how their online interactions influenced their political views and engagement through these interviews. For example, one participant described feeling increasingly isolated from opposing viewpoints, while another spoke about the empowerment they felt connecting with like-minded individuals.

This combination of quantitative data and qualitative insights allowed the researcher to explore causal mechanisms beyond simple correlations. The researcher could identify broader social and economic factors influencing online behaviour by employing retroduction—an inference method that moves from observed effects back to the underlying causes. The findings highlighted the complexities of how social media shapes political identities while also acknowledging that individual experiences vary widely.

Key Differences Highlighted

These case studies illustrate the notable differences between constructivist and critical realist approaches:

The constructivist study prioritises rich, individual narratives, seeking to understand the unique experiences of immigrant women and how they make sense of their interactions with the healthcare system.

The critical realist study aims to uncover underlying mechanisms that drive observable outcomes, providing a broader understanding of political polarisation in the context of social media.

Both approaches possess distinct strengths and weaknesses, making them suitable for addressing different research questions. Researchers often find value in integrating aspects from both frameworks to provide a more comprehensive understanding of social issues.

Conclusion

The specific research context and questions influence the choice between constructivism and critical realism. Constructivism is particularly effective for exploring how individuals interpret their experiences, while critical realism seeks to identify causal structures that can inform generalisable theories. Researchers can enhance their analysis of complex social phenomena by recognising the balance between subjective meanings and objective realities. Ultimately, this integration contributes to a richer understanding of our world's intricate processes.

METHODOLOGICAL IMPLICATIONS OF CONSTRUCTIVIST AND CRITICAL REALIST PERSPECTIVES

As we explore constructivism and critical realism further, it becomes clear that these philosophical approaches significantly shape the entire research process—from the initial design to the final interpretation of findings. Understanding these implications is essential for researchers who aim to conduct rigorous and ethical studies within the post-positivist paradigm(Shannon-Baker, 2023).

Constructivism emphasises that reality is created through social interactions and shared meanings. This perspective naturally lends itself to qualitative methodologies. When researchers adopt a constructivist stance, they often choose methods that focus on an in-depth understanding of individual experiences and interpretations (Fodouop Kouam, 2024). For instance, ethnographic studies allow researchers to immerse themselves in the social context being studied, gathering rich data through participant observation and interviews. Imagine a researcher living within a community to research health beliefs; this immersive approach can produce detailed accounts of how individuals perceive health and illness, revealing the complexities of their cultural practices.

In this approach, the process of meaning-making is central. Data analysis involves identifying themes and patterns within the narratives shared by participants. For example, if the researcher is studying the experiences of immigrant women navigating healthcare, they may uncover themes related to cultural barriers and trust in healthcare providers. This emphasis on interpretation enables researchers to draw out subtle nuances in experiences that quantitative methods could miss.

On the other hand, critical realism offers a counterpoint by asserting that an objective reality exists, even if social contexts shape our understanding of it. It recognises the complexities of social phenomena and aims to uncover the underlying structures and mechanisms that drive observable events (Shannon-Baker, 2023). For example, if researchers study educational inequality, they may examine test scores and investigate funding disparities between schools and the societal factors influencing these inequities.

Critical realist research often embraces a mixed-methods approach, integrating both qualitative and quantitative data. This combination allows for a comprehensive understanding of the issues at hand (Fletcher, 2017). For instance, a critical realist study may start with quantitative data to establish a correlation between socioeconomic status and academic performance while conducting interviews to understand the lived experiences of students affected by these factors. By linking the numerical data with personal narratives, researchers can uncover deeper insights into the challenges faced by students from differing backgrounds.

The implications for research design are significant. Constructivist researchers frequently employ emergent designs, where the research questions evolve as insights are gained throughout the study. This flexibility allows for a more in-depth exploration of the phenomenon at hand (Fodouop Kouam, 2024). In contrast, critical realism favours a more structured approach, often starting with specific hypotheses that can be tested through rigorous data collection (Fletcher, 2017).

Balancing Perspectives

Choosing between constructivism and critical realism is not merely about selecting a preferred method; it reflects deeper ontological (beliefs about the nature of reality) and epistemological (beliefs about knowledge) commitments. Researchers should consider their research question and the nature of the phenomenon being studied.

For instance, a constructivist approach is well-suited for questions focused on understanding subjective experiences, while critical realism is ideal for investigating causal mechanisms and testing theories.

Moreover, many research studies can benefit from integrating both perspectives. The complementary nature of constructivism and critical realism suggests that a mixed-methods approach, which combines qualitative and quantitative techniques, often provides a richer understanding of social phenomena. For example, a study on climate change could incorporate qualitative interviews to uncover personal experiences of displacement alongside quantitative data on environmental changes.

This comprehensive strategy helps ensure that researchers capture the complexities of human experience while identifying broader societal patterns. By thoughtfully combining methods, researchers can gain deeper insights into the intricate interplay of individual experiences and underlying social forces that shape our world.

Conclusion

In conclusion, the methodological implications of constructivist and critical realist perspectives are far-reaching. By thoughtfully considering the strengths and limitations of each approach, researchers can design studies that effectively address their research questions. Integrating diverse methods enhances the credibility, validity, and overall contribution of research, paving the way for a more nuanced understanding of the complexities of social phenomena. Ultimately, this flexible and robust approach enriches the field of social science, advancing our knowledge of the intricate processes that define our society.

Table 16: *Methodological Implications of Constructivist and Critical Realist Perspectives*

Aspect	Constructivism	Critical Realism
Core Idea	Reality is socially constructed through interactions and shared meanings.	An objective reality exists, influenced by social structures and human interpretation.
Research Focus	Emphasises understanding individual experiences and meanings.	Aims to uncover causal mechanisms and underlying structures that drive observable phenomena.
Methodology	Qualitative methods such as ethnography and grounded theory are used to explore rich, contextual data.	Employs mixed-methods approaches, integrating quantitative data with qualitative insights for depth.
Data Analysis	Involves thematic analysis to identify patterns and nuances from participant narratives.	Utilises statistical analysis alongside qualitative interpretation to understand complex relationships.
Strengths	Captures the richness of human experiences and provides deep insights.	Explains causal relationships and reveals underlying social structures shaping phenomena.
Limitations	Challenges in generalisability; findings may be context-specific.	Difficulties in establishing clear causal links; may overlook individual agency in favour of structural factors.
Ethical Considerations	It requires reflexivity to mitigate researcher bias and emphasises building trust with participants.	Highlights the need for transparency in methodology and ethical treatment of data and participants.

CHAPTER 5: ADDRESSING RESEARCHER BIAS AND CONTEXT

RECOGNISING AND MITIGATING RESEARCHER BIAS

Researcher bias is a common challenge in all research paradigms and can subtly influence every stage of the research process—from forming research questions to interpreting findings. Recognising and addressing these biases is crucial for ensuring the validity and trustworthiness of research (Schweizer et al., 2016).

Types of Researcher Bias

One significant type of bias is **confirmation bias**, favouring information that supports pre-existing beliefs while discounting contradictory evidence. For instance, if a researcher believes a new educational programme is effective, they may focus only on positive feedback and ignore negative outcomes. Researchers can implement rigorous data collection protocols to combat this bias, actively seek contradictory evidence, and engage in peer reviews to gain external perspectives (Suzuki & Yamamoto, 2021).

Sampling bias is another critical concern. This arises when the sample does not accurately represent the population being studied. For example, if a study on public health is conducted only among college students, it may not reflect the views of older adults or other demographic groups. Employing proper sampling techniques like random sampling can help mitigate this issue, ensuring that findings are more generalisable (S. W. Chen, Keglovits, Devine, & Stark, 2021).

Observer bias, sometimes called experimenter bias, occurs when the researcher's expectations influence their observations.

In qualitative research, if a researcher expects participants to have positive experiences with treatment, they may unconsciously interpret ambiguous responses in that light. Implementing **blinding procedures**, where researchers are unaware of participant group assignments, can reduce this bias (Mahtani, Spencer, Brassey, & Heneghan, 2018).

Another consideration is **funding/sponsorship bias**, where the funding source could influence the research focus or outcomes. Researchers should transparently disclose funding sources to enable readers to assess potential influences on their findings. Maintaining scientific integrity is paramount, even under pressure to align results with funders' interests (Lexchin, 2012).

Cognitive biases also play a significant role. These biases, such as anchoring bias (relying too heavily on initial information), stereotyping and heuristics (systematic errors in judgment and decision-making that occur when people rely on mental shortcuts), can affect various stages of the research process. New researchers are encouraged to engage in self-reflection, using tools like reflective journaling to identify their biases (Spiliopoulos & Hertwig, 2024).

Cultivating Reflexivity

Creating a culture of reflexivity—critical self-reflection on the researcher's biases and assumptions—is essential. Researchers should regularly examine how their backgrounds influence their research choices and interpretations (Korstjens & Moser, 2017). For instance, when conducting interviews, a researcher could reflect on their personal experiences related to the topic and how these could shape their understanding.

Contextual Factors

Recognising the influence of contextual factors is also vital. The social, cultural, and economic settings in which research occurs can shape outcomes and interpretations.

Researchers should document these factors to provide a clearer context for their findings. For example, describing the dynamic in a community study helps others understand how context may influence results.

Promoting Transparency

Lastly, fostering transparency is key to reducing bias. Researchers should clearly document their methods, data collection processes, and study limitations. Sharing research materials and findings helps facilitate scrutiny and can identify potential biases. Adherence to ethical practices, such as informed consent and participant confidentiality, is fundamental for conducting responsible research (Korstjens & Moser, 2017).

Case Study: Navigating Bias: Ensuring Integrity in Research at Crestwood University

At Crestwood University, Dr Anna, an enthusiastic researcher, sought to investigate the impact of community-based health programmes on residents' overall wellbeing. Understanding the significance of addressing researcher bias, she aimed to ensure the validity and trustworthiness of her findings throughout the research process.

<u>Recognising and Mitigating Researcher Bias</u>

Dr Anna was acutely aware that researcher bias could subtly influence every stage of her study, from forming research questions to interpreting the final results. She recognised several types of bias that could affect her research:

Confirmation Bias: Dr Anna understood that she could unconsciously favour information supporting her beliefs. If she believed the community health programme was effective, she may focus more on positive feedback and ignore negative responses.

She implemented rigorous data collection protocols to counteract this bias and actively sought contradictory evidence. She also engaged in peer reviews, inviting colleagues to critique her approach and contribute external perspectives.

Sampling Bias: Understanding the implications of sampling bias, Dr Anna aimed to create a representative sample of the community. She recognised that conducting her study solely among a specific demographic, such as college students, would not accurately reflect the views of broader populations like older adults or low-income families. To mitigate this concern, she employed proper sampling techniques, including random sampling, ensuring that her findings would be more generalisable.

Observer Bias: Dr Anna was sensitive to the risk of observer bias, which occurs when a researcher's expectations influence their observations. In her qualitative interviews, she aimed not to let her preconceptions about the programme's success taint her interpretation of participant responses. To reduce this risk, she implemented blinding procedures, where assistants conducted the interviews without revealing her expectations to the participants.

Funding Bias: Acknowledging that the funding source could impact research outcomes, Dr Anna made it a priority to consult her funding bodies with transparency. By disclosing funding sources in her publications, she allowed readers to assess potential influences on her research conclusions, reinforcing her commitment to maintaining scientific integrity.

Cognitive Biases: Dr Anna recognised the role cognitive biases, such as anchoring bias and overconfidence bias, could play in her work. As a new researcher, she committed to self-reflection, using methods like reflective journaling to identify and confront her biases regularly.

Cultivating Reflexivity

Dr Anna was determined to cultivate a culture of reflexivity within her research. She understood that critical self-reflection on her biases and assumptions was essential for conducting trustworthy research. For example, during her interviews with participants, she often reflected on her personal experiences related to health and wellbeing, consciously acknowledging how these views could shape her understanding of the topic.

Contextual Factors: Recognising Their Influence

Recognising the impact of contextual factors was also vital to Dr Anna's research. The social, cultural, and economic environments in which her study took place could shape her outcomes and interpretations. Therefore, she diligently documented these factors, providing context for her findings. For instance, by describing the dynamics of the community where the health programme was implemented, she allowed others to evaluate how these contextual elements could influence the results.

Promoting Transparency in Research

Dr Anna emphasised that transparency was crucial in minimising bias and enhancing the integrity of her research. She meticulously documented her research methods, data collection processes, and any limitations encountered throughout the study. By sharing her research materials and findings with her academic community, Dr Anna facilitated scrutiny and identification of potential biases, ensuring collaborative integrity.

Conclusion: Upholding Integrity in Research

After months of dedicated work, Dr Anna completed her research and synthesised her findings. She revealed valuable insights into how community health programmes impacted residents' wellbeing, highlighting the importance of addressing social and contextual factors. In her presentation at Crestwood University, Dr Anna demonstrated how recognising and mitigating researcher bias drives the credibility of qualitative research. By advocating for reflexivity, transparency, and ethical practices, she underscored the necessity of maintaining integrity in research. Dr Anna's journey exemplified the importance of being vigilant against biases and understanding the influence of context on research outcomes. She contributed significantly to advancing academic discussions and informed practices within community health initiatives through her commitment to these principles. Her work inspired fellow researchers to embrace similar ethical considerations in their inquiries, promoting a collective pursuit of rigorous and trustworthy research outcomes.

Conclusion

In conclusion, effectively addressing researcher bias requires a multifaceted approach. By understanding the types of biases that can occur, employing strategies to minimise their influence, engaging in self-reflection, recognising contextual factors, and adhering to ethical guidelines, researchers can enhance the rigour and impact of their studies. The commitment to transparency and self-awareness enables researchers to produce reliable and valuable contributions to knowledge in their fields, reinforcing the pursuit of objective understanding amidst the complexities of social research.

Table 17: Recognising and Mitigating Researcher Bias

Type of Bias	Description	Mitigation Strategies
Confirmation Bias	The tendency to favour information that supports existing beliefs while discounting contradictory evidence.	- Employ rigorous data collection protocols. - Seek contrasting evidence. - Engage in peer reviews for external perspectives.
Sampling Bias	When the sample does not accurately represent population studied.	Use sampling techniques, like random sampling for representativeness.
Observer Bias	The influence of the researcher's expectations on their observations and interpretations.	Implement blinding procedures where researchers are unaware of group assignments.
Funding Bias	The influence of funding sources on research focus or outcomes.	Disclose funding sources transparently.
Cognitive Biases	Inherent biases in human thinking that affect the research process.	- Engage in self-reflection tools i.e journalling.
Reflexivity	The practice of critically examining one's own biases and assumptions throughout the research process.	- Integrate reflexive practices into the research design, openly discussing biases and assumptions.

THE IMPORTANCE
OF REFLEXIVITY
IN RESEARCH

As we delve deeper into research methods, one critical aspect that emerges is reflexivity. Reflexivity involves the researcher's ongoing self-reflection regarding their own biases, assumptions, values, and perspectives and how these may shape the research process and findings. It goes beyond acknowledging bias; it requires a conscious engagement with how personal experiences and social contexts influence research design, data collection, and interpretation (Korstjens & Moser, 2017).

Understanding reflexivity is essential. No matter how much researchers strive for objectivity, they are inherently situated within specific social, cultural, and political contexts. These contexts inform their worldviews and how they interpret data. Without a commitment to reflexivity, researchers risk imposing their own perspectives onto the participants and the subject matter, leading to biased conclusions.

Illustrative Example: Consider a researcher studying the experiences of undocumented immigrants. If the researcher strongly supports immigration rights, their interactions may unintentionally lead participants to confirm their pre-existing beliefs. Conversely, a researcher with negative views on immigration may unintentionally push participants to downplay or hide aspects of their experiences that don't fit those beliefs. A reflexive approach involves critically examining these potential biases and actively working to minimise their impact.

Reflexivity in Practice

Reflexivity is a continuous process rather than a one-time event.

Researchers should engage in regular self-reflection, perhaps through journaling, and seek feedback from colleagues who can offer diverse perspectives. For instance, a researcher may keep a diary documenting their emotional responses during interviews to recognise how these feelings influence their interpretations.

Additionally, reflexivity encompasses methodological choices. For example, a qualitative researcher using a narrative approach should be cautious about giving undue weight to certain voices while marginalising others. This awareness helps in making more balanced choices throughout the research process.

Ethical Considerations

The ethical dimensions of reflexivity are also crucial. Researchers should consider the power dynamics at play, especially when working with vulnerable populations.

For instance:

Informed Consent: Ensuring that participants understand their rights and the research purpose.

Confidentiality: Protecting participants' identities is paramount, particularly when discussing sensitive topics. Being aware of how power imbalances could affect participants' responses is essential. A researcher in a position of authority may find that participants feel pressured to answer in a way that aligns with the researcher's expectations, potentially leading to skewed data.

Conclusion

In conclusion, reflexivity is not merely a methodological technique—it's an ethical and epistemological imperative. It requires a constant critical examination of one's own positionality, biases, and assumptions, along with a commitment to transparency. By engaging in this ongoing process, researchers can enhance the rigor and validity of their work while contributing to a more nuanced understanding of social phenomena.

The practice of reflexivity is fundamental to producing research that is not only methodologically sound but also ethically responsible. Ultimately, the goal is not to eliminate bias entirely—an almost impossible task—but to acknowledge and manage its influence to the best of our ability. This commitment to reflexivity fosters research findings that are robust and reliable and contributes to creating more equitable social outcomes.

UNDERSTANDING CONTEXTUAL FACTORS AND THEIR INFLUENCE ON RESEARCH FINDINGS

I n exploring researcher bias, it's crucial to delve into the importance of contextual factors in shaping research findings. Neglecting the research context is akin to studying a single leaf and claiming to understand the entire forest. Contextual factors—including social, cultural, historical, political, and economic environments—influence every stage of the research process, from formulating research questions to interpreting results (Spiliopoulos & Hertwig, 2024).

Key Contextual Factors

Socio-Cultural Environment

The socio-cultural context profoundly affects both participants and researchers (Huesemann, 2002). For instance, a study examining gender roles conducted in a patriarchal society may yield different insights compared to one in a more egalitarian culture. Cultural norms dictate how individuals express themselves and their willingness to disclose sensitive information. **Mitigation**: Employing culturally sensitive methods, such as using competent translators who understand cultural nuances and adopting participatory approaches that involve community members in the research, can help address these disparities. This practice ensures that the research is respectful and meaningful to the community involved.

Historical Context

Historical events significantly shape present attitudes and beliefs, providing an essential background for understanding social phenomena (De Vos et al., 2005). For example, a study on political views could yield divergent outcomes if conducted during political stability versus periods of upheaval or revolution. History provides a context for current perceptions and behaviours. **Mitigation**: Researchers should investigate historical trends and consult relevant documents to provide richer context. For instance, analysing how past policies influenced current societal attitudes on healthcare can lead to deeper insights into community health behaviours and beliefs.

Political Context

The political environment can significantly affect research dynamics. In authoritarian regimes, certain topics may be sensitive or restricted, influencing the data collection process. Researchers need to be aware of how political structures impact access to information, participant responses, and the dissemination of findings (Fletcher, 2017). **Mitigation**: Understanding the political landscape helps guide responsible data management and reporting practices. Researchers should consider potential ethical dilemmas when engaging with sensitive topics, ensuring that they protect participants and maintain academic integrity.

Economic Context

Economic conditions influence access to resources and participation in research (Kaufman & Ramarao, 2005). For instance, a study on healthcare access may reveal different insights when conducted in affluent communities compared to impoverished ones, where disparities in access to services can affect participant responses. **Mitigation**: Acknowledging economic factors is crucial for interpreting findings. Researchers should examine how participants' economic backgrounds shape their experiences and perspectives, allowing for a more comprehensive understanding of the issues.

Research Setting

Participants' specific research location and characteristics play a crucial role in the research process (Handley et al., 2018). For instance, studying classroom dynamics in a small rural school may yield insights about community engagement that differ from those in a large urban school, where diverse socio-economic factors come into play. **Mitigation**: Establishing trust and rapport with participants is key to successful research. Techniques such as obtaining informed consent, ensuring confidentiality, and being transparent about the research purpose can help build strong relationships, leading to richer data collection.

Methodological Choices and Context

The research context influences the selection of qualitative or quantitative methods. Some situations may favour quantitative approaches that provide broad trends, while others are better suited for qualitative methods that deeply explore personal stories. Researchers need to think carefully about their choices:

Example: A researcher investigating community health issues may find qualitative methods beneficial in capturing the personal experiences of residents. Meanwhile, another researcher examining national health statistics could focus more on quantitative methods for broader trends.

Navigating Context: Understanding Researcher Bias and Contextual Factors at Sunnyvale University

At Sunnyvale University, Dr Lily initiated a project to investigate the impact of community health initiatives on disadvantaged groups in her local area. Acknowledging the importance of contextual factors was critical for understanding the complexities of her research findings.

Recognising and Mitigating Researcher Bias

Dr Lily understood that researcher bias could influence every stage of her study, from formulating research questions to interpreting results. She recognised various types of bias that could compromise the integrity of her work:

Confirmation Bias: As she explored the effectiveness of health programmes, Dr Lily recognised the potential to favour information that supported her existing beliefs. For instance, if she perceived a specific programme as effective, she may disproportionately consider positive feedback while overlooking negative responses. To address this, she implemented rigorous data collection protocols, actively sought contradictory evidence, and involved colleagues in peer reviews to obtain external perspectives.

Sampling Bias: Dr Lily was aware of the significance of sampling bias, especially when studying disadvantaged groups. The findings could not accurately reflect the broader population if her sample included primarily participants from affluent backgrounds. She employed random sampling techniques to ensure diverse demographics were represented, thereby correctly reflecting the experiences of those affected by social disparities.

Observer Bias: Dr Lily recognised that her expectations could influence how she interpreted participants' responses. To alleviate this risk, she established blinding procedures, enabling research assistants to conduct interviews without disclosing her expectations.

Understanding Contextual Factors: The Role of Social Norms and Systemic Prejudice

As Dr Lily designed her study, she prioritised understanding contextual factors that shape participants and research outcomes.

Socio-Cultural Environment: The socio-cultural context influences how disadvantaged groups perceive health initiatives. In communities where cultural norms may discourage open discussions about mental health, participants could hesitate to share experiences. Dr Lily employed culturally sensitive methods, collaborating with translators familiar with local dialects to navigate these challenges effectively.

Historical Context: Dr Lily recognised that historical events and systemic prejudice could shape current attitudes towards healthcare. She considered how past experiences with healthcare systems, including discrimination or lack of access, could influence present behaviours and beliefs. By analysing historical documents and trends, she sought to provide a rich context for her findings.

Political Context: The political environment where she conducted her research significantly impacted her study. Dr Lily understood that certain health-related topics may be sensitive due to existing political tensions. Awareness of these factors was crucial in navigating ethical dilemmas and ensuring participant protection throughout data collection.

Research Setting: The characteristics of the research setting influenced Dr Lily's study. For instance, examining health dynamics in a small rural community may yield different insights compared to a large urban setting, where systemic issues and socio-economic diversity are prevalent. Establishing trust with participants was essential, so she prioritised informed consent and confidentiality.

Methodological Choices and Context

Dr Lily deliberated in her methodological choices, recognising that both qualitative and quantitative methods offer valuable insights depending on the context. For example, when exploring community health issues, qualitative methods such as interviews could capture personal narratives, while quantitative methods could reveal broader trends in health outcomes.

Conclusion: The Importance of Context in Research

After completing her research and analysing the data, Dr Lily presented her findings at Sunnyvale University, illustrating how contextual factors influence the experiences of disadvantaged groups with community health initiatives.

Her study highlighted the necessity of recognising these factors to produce accurate and meaningful findings. Dr Lily's understanding of the complexities surrounding her participants' lives informed recommendations for improved health interventions.

By advocating for a comprehensive research approach that acknowledges the importance of context, Dr Lily encouraged her colleagues to engage with the intricacies of social diversity and systemic issues in their own studies.

Dr Lily's research illustrated the significance of acknowledging contextual factors in comprehending the experiences of disadvantaged groups regarding community health initiatives. She presented a comprehensive view of the subject by integrating insights into socio-cultural norms, historical influences, and systemic prejudice.

In summary, Dr Lily's work at Sunnyvale University reinforced the role of context in qualitative research. She demonstrated that understanding human experiences necessitates a thorough engagement with the settings and conditions that shape those experiences.

Conclusion

Addressing contextual factors is essential for producing credible and reliable research. Researchers should critically evaluate their research context, actively seeking to understand how these elements influence their findings. This requires reflexivity—not just regarding personal biases but also regarding the social, cultural, historical, political, and economic factors at play.

By acknowledging and addressing these contextual influences, researchers enhance the validity and generalisability of their work, leading to a more nuanced understanding of social phenomena. This commitment to contextual awareness not only clarifies the research process but also promotes responsible and ethical research practices. Ultimately, understanding the interplay between research and context is vital for advancing knowledge and fostering equity in the social sciences.

TRANSPARENCY AND ETHICAL CONSIDERATIONS IN RESEARCH

Building on our discussion of reflexivity and contextual awareness, it's essential to explore the vital roles of **transparency** and **ethical considerations** in the research process. Understanding these elements is essential for conducting trustworthy and responsible research, which enhances the validity of findings and fosters public trust in the scientific community (Korstjens & Moser, 2017).

Importance of Transparency

Transparency in research is about being open and clear regarding all study aspects. It goes beyond merely presenting findings and covers a comprehensive disclosure of the entire research process, including (Korstjens & Moser, 2017):

Research Design: Clearly explaining how the study was structured is crucial. This includes detailing the methods used to select participants and the data collection techniques employed. For instance, if a study collects data through interviews, the researcher should specify how participants were chosen and whether any criteria were used to select a diverse or representative sample.

Methodology: It is essential to describe the specific procedures followed during the research. This includes outlining any tools or instruments used for data collection, such as surveys or interview guides, along with their development and validation. For example, if a questionnaire measures stress levels, explaining how the questions were formulated and tested for reliability will strengthen the study's credibility.

Limitations: Acknowledging any research design or methodology weaknesses is crucial for transparency. This means being upfront about potential issues that may affect results. For instance, if a study uses a small sample size, this should be noted as a limitation that could impact generalisability (the extent to which findings apply to broader contexts).

Open sharing of data while ensuring participant privacy forms another critical aspect of transparency. Providing access to the data collected allows other researchers to replicate the study, verify findings, and build further research on the initial work. While confidentiality must be respected, sharing aggregated data formats can facilitate transparency without compromising individual anonymity.

Ethical Considerations

Ethical considerations are at the core of responsible research practices. Key aspects encompass:

Informed Consent: It is vital that participants fully understand the purpose of the study and their rights before agreeing to participate. Researchers should communicate the study processes clearly, including potential risks and benefits. This sets the foundation for an ethical research relationship (Kaufman & Ramarao, 2005).

Confidentiality: Protecting participants' identities and sensitive information cannot be overstated. Researchers need to implement robust data management practices, such as anonymising data, to safeguard against any potential breaches of confidentiality (Kaufman & Ramarao, 2005). For example, using aggregate data rather than individual identifiers protects participants' privacy when reporting research findings.

Community Impact: Researchers should consider the broader societal implications of their findings. Engaging with communities affected by the research ensures that the study addresses their needs and concerns. This may involve community-based participatory research, where participants help shape the research design and focus (Kaufman & Ramarao, 2005).

Furthermore, researchers should be mindful of potential **conflicts of interest**. These can arise from various sources, such as funding bodies or personal affiliations, that may influence the study's direction and outcomes. Clearly disclosing any potential biases helps maintain the integrity of the research process and allows readers to assess the work's validity critically (Lexchin, 2012).

Conclusion

In conclusion, transparency and ethical considerations are fundamental to producing high-quality, credible, and socially responsible research. These elements should be deeply integrated into the research process and are interconnected with reflexivity and contextual awareness.

While prioritising transparency demands ongoing reflection and commitment, it fosters an environment of trust, accountability, and the pursuit of knowledge. It encourages researchers to present their findings honestly, without exaggeration or misrepresentation. This is not just about adhering to academic rules; it involves cultivating a culture of ethical responsibility where researchers thoughtfully consider the wider implications of their work.

By ensuring both transparency and ethical integrity, we can contribute positively to society, advancing knowledge while promoting social justice. Engaging in this ethical research practice helps create a stronger foundation for credible findings, ultimately leading to a more informed and just understanding of the complexities within our social world.

CHOOSING THE APPROPRIATE PARADIGM FOR YOUR RESEARCH

Selecting a research paradigm is a crucial decision that influences every aspect of the research process, from formulating questions to interpreting findings. It's not just about which method you prefer but about ensuring your chosen framework aligns with your research goals. Understanding the differences between paradigms helps researchers avoid flawed methodologies and biased interpretations.

Key Considerations in Paradigm Selection

1. Ontological Commitments

Researchers should first consider their beliefs about the nature of reality, known as ontology (Shannon-Baker, 2023). Do you believe in an objective reality independent of observers (a realist perspective typical of positivism), or do you see reality as subjective and constructed through social interactions (a constructivist perspective)? For instance, if you are studying how people perceive family structures, your approach will differ based on whether you think there's a universal definition of family or see its meaning as fluid and culturally specific.

2. Epistemological Perspectives

Next, consider your stance on knowledge—epistemology. Positivists typically believe knowledge can be achieved through unbiased observation, whereas post-positivists recognise that our experiences influence our understanding (Shannon-Baker, 2023). For example, if you're investigating the impact of social media on mental health, a positivist would focus on measuring data from surveys. At the same time, a post-positivist could conduct interviews to explore personal experiences and feelings.

3. Methodological Choices

Methodology encompasses the techniques used to collect and analyse data. Positivist research often utilises quantitative methods like experiments and surveys, focusing on generalisation from large samples. In contrast, post-positivist research embraces both qualitative and quantitative methods to gain a richer understanding (De Vos et al., 2005). For example, if exploring the effectiveness of a new teaching method, a positivist may compare test scores. At the same time, a post-positivist would examine both scores and students' thoughts on the method.

4. Research Questions

The specific research question guides the choice of paradigm (De Vos et al., 2005). A question seeking causal relationships, such as "Does social media use decrease adolescent self-esteem?" fits well with positivist methods. In contrast, a question like "How do adolescents perceive their self-esteem in relation to social media?" aligns more with a constructivist approach.

5. Practical Constraints

Practical factors, such as available resources and access to participants, also play a significant role (Rutkowski et al., 2024). For example, conducting a large-scale quantitative study may be impractical if funding or time is limited. Similarly, the characteristics of the target population may dictate the methods used.

Reflexivity and Critical Awareness

Researchers should remain aware of their values and biases throughout the process. Complete objectivity is often unattainable. By reflecting on how personal beliefs may shape the research, you can gain insights into potential influences on your findings (Korstjens & Moser, 2017). For example, if a researcher strongly believes in the benefits of social media, this could impact how they interpret data regarding its effects.

Engaging in transparent documentation of methodological choices and acknowledging potential biases are also critical. A comprehensive report detailing your approach helps others understand the context and trust the findings.

Conclusion

In conclusion, choosing the appropriate research paradigm is a significant decision that requires thoughtful consideration of your ontological and epistemological beliefs, research questions, and practical constraints. While adhering to a specific paradigm provides structure, researchers should remain flexible, allowing for adaptations as the study evolves.

Researchers can enrich their investigations by integrating elements from different paradigms and provide a nuanced understanding of complex social phenomena. This balanced approach reflects a commitment to rigorous scholarship, enhancing your research's quality and impact. Ultimately, the goal is to contribute meaningfully to knowledge, using ethical research practices guided by a well-articulated and consistent research paradigm.

INTEGRATING POSITIVIST AND POST-POSITIVIST APPROACHES

As we explore research methodologies, it's essential to recognise that the choice of a research paradigm profoundly shapes the entire research process. Understanding the intricacies of positivism and post-positivism reveals opportunities to bridge the two approaches, creating a more comprehensive view of complex social phenomena (Busetto et al., 2020).

The Power of Mixed Methods

Mixed methods research stands out as a valuable strategy that combines both quantitative and qualitative approaches. This integration allows researchers to leverage the strengths of each paradigm, addressing their limitations and enhancing the richness of the findings (Shiyanbola et al., 2021).

For example, imagine a study investigating the impact of social media on political engagement. A positivist researcher may analyse large datasets to identify statistical correlations between social media use and voting behaviour. While this quantitative data can highlight trends, it often overlooks the nuances of individual experiences. Conversely, a post-positivist researcher could conduct in-depth interviews to explore how individuals perceive online interactions and how they shape their political identities. By combining these methods, the study can reveal trends and the personal stories behind those trends, providing a deeper understanding of the relationship between social media and political engagement.

Benefits of Integration

There are several key advantages to integrating these approaches:

Comprehensive Understanding: Researchers can develop a more holistic understanding of the research topic using qualitative and quantitative data. This dual perspective helps uncover the complexities and layers within social phenomena that a single method may miss (De Vos et al., 2005).

Triangulation: This technique strengthens the validity of research findings by confirming results through different methods. For instance, if both survey data and interview insights lead to similar conclusions about a programme's effectiveness, researchers can have greater confidence in their results (Patton, 1999).

Flexibility: An integrative approach allows researchers to adapt to the research context and objectives, choosing methods that best fit their specific questions. This adaptability can lead to more effective and relevant research outcomes (Keyter & Roos, 2015).

Challenges of Integration

While the benefits of combining positivist and post-positivist approaches are substantial, researchers should also navigate certain challenges:

Methodological Complexity: Integrating different methods requires careful planning. Researchers should ensure that the quantitative and qualitative components complement each other, which can demand considerable time and resources (Stern et al., 2020).

Ethical Considerations: Researchers should obtain informed consent from participants for both data types, maintaining ethical standards throughout the process.

Transparency about potential biases is also essential to uphold the integrity of the research (Stern et al., 2020).

Analysing Diverse Data: The analysis of mixed methods can be intricate. Researchers should clearly articulate the integration strategy, addressing any inconsistencies between quantitative and qualitative findings (Stern et al., 2020).

Conclusion

In conclusion, choosing to integrate positivist and post-positivist approaches is driven by the specific research question and context. While constructivist methods are excellent for exploring subjective experiences, critical realism is better suited for identifying causal mechanisms and testing theories. By thoughtfully incorporating both approaches, researchers can develop richer insights and contribute more meaningfully to our understanding of social issues.

This integrated method exemplifies the evolving landscape of social science research, fostering a deeper comprehension of the complexities of human experience. As researchers continue to embrace mixed methods, they can effectively respond to the intricate social questions of our time, ensuring rigorous, valid, and impactful findings.

FUTURE DIRECTIONS IN RESEARCH METHODOLOGY

As we reflect on the complexities of research design in the social sciences, we focus on future research methodology directions. The landscape of inquiry is evolving rapidly, driven by advancements in technology and the increasing availability of diverse data sources. Researchers should adapt to these changes to enhance the rigour and relevance of their work.

The Rise of Big Data

One of the most significant trends shaping research methodology is the emergence of **big data**. Characterised by its volume, velocity, variety, veracity, and value (the five Vs), big data presents both remarkable opportunities and notable challenges for researchers (Saeed & Husamaldin, 2021).

Opportunities: The sheer volume of data available—from social media interactions to sensor data from devices—can provide profound insights into social behaviours and trends. For example, researchers can analyse vast datasets from social media platforms to gauge public sentiment during elections, gaining real-time insights into how individuals express their political opinions online (Matilda, 2016).

Challenges: However, managing and interpreting such large datasets requires sophisticated computational tools and a robust understanding of statistical modelling techniques. Researchers should be equipped to handle issues related to data quality, such as missing values and potential biases in data collection. For instance, if data are primarily sourced from one demographic group, the findings may not accurately reflect the general population's views. Ethical implications concerning privacy and data security further complicate the landscape. Researchers should navigate these concerns diligently, ensuring that personal data is anonymised and secure (Wang, Chen, Schifano, Wu, & Yan, 2016).

Integrating Qualitative Methods

While big data offers extensive quantitative insights, it often lacks the depth needed to understand human behaviour's complexities fully (García Portilla, 2022). This is where qualitative methods become essential. Researchers can uncover the "why" and "how" behind the patterns observed in quantitative data by integrating qualitative research techniques, such as interviews and focus groups.

Example: A researcher may conduct in-depth interviews with users after identifying a correlation between social media usage and political engagement via quantitative analysis. This qualitative component would explore how individuals interpret online interactions and how these shape their political views and identities. Such insights can reveal motivations, fears, and personal narratives that numerical data alone cannot capture.

Methodological Innovations

Integrating qualitative and quantitative methods is increasingly common, reflecting a **mixed-methods approach**. This strategy allows researchers to tap into the strengths of both paradigms, enhancing the overall rigour and depth of their studies (Shannon-Baker, 2023).

Example: In a study on the effectiveness of a community health programme, researchers may start with quantitative surveys measuring health outcomes for participants. Following this, they could conduct qualitative interviews to delve into the experiences of those involved, discovering barriers to access or unforeseen benefits not evident in the survey data alone. This combination enriches the findings, providing a well-rounded perspective on the programme's impact.

Emerging Technologies

Advancements in technology, such as **virtual reality (VR)** and **augmented reality (AR)**, open exciting new avenues for qualitative and quantitative data collection (Syed Mohammad, 2009).

Example: In researching social behaviours, a researcher could use virtual reality to simulate social scenarios, allowing participants to engage in lifelike interactions. For instance, VR can create environments replicating real-world social situations, providing researchers with a unique opportunity to observe interactions that may be difficult to study otherwise. However, this also raises ethical questions about informed consent and the potential psychological impact of immersive experiences, necessitating careful ethical review and consideration.

Ethical Considerations

As research methodologies evolve, ethical implications remain a priority. Researchers should develop responsible and transparent practices to address participant rights and data usage issues. This includes:

Informed Consent: Ensuring participants fully know the research purpose, methods, and potential risks involved is essential for ethical integrity.

Confidentiality: Safeguarding participants' identities and sensitive information strengthens trust and encourages honest participation.

Community consultations can also give researchers insights into participants' needs and concerns, ensuring the research is responsive and relevant.

Conclusion

In conclusion, the future of research methodology in the social sciences is filled with opportunities and challenges. The rise of big data, technological advancements, and the integration of mixed methods are transforming how researchers engage with social inquiries. By thoughtfully considering their methodology, researchers can generate profound insights into complex social phenomena.

Understanding the strengths and limitations of each approach is vital in making informed methodological choices. This flexibility facilitates thorough analysis and fosters a deeper respect for the intricacies of the social world. Researchers who integrate various methodologies can achieve richer, more comprehensive findings, ultimately contributing to a more thorough understanding of the complexities of human behaviour and societal change.

Through continuous critical reflection, collaborative efforts, and methodological innovation, researchers can effectively navigate the evolving landscape of social science research. This commitment will enable them to provide meaningful contributions that enhance knowledge and promote social progress.

CRITICAL REFLECTION ON THE ROLE OF PARADIGMS IN SHAPING RESEARCH

As we reflect on the previous chapters, we've laid the groundwork for understanding how research paradigms influence the design and interpretation of social science research. By examining both positivism and post-positivism, we can see how these frameworks provide distinct but complementary approaches to inquiry.

Understanding the Paradigm Influence

Choosing a research paradigm is not a trivial decision; it shapes every aspect of the research journey, from the initial formulation of questions to the final interpretation of results. Researchers should consider their ontological (beliefs about reality) and epistemological (beliefs about knowledge) commitments. For instance, if a researcher believes in an objective reality (common in positivism), they may focus on quantifiable variables and statistical analysis to establish **generalisable** laws. In contrast, a researcher who embraces constructivism would explore how social interactions shape individual experiences, utilising qualitative methods to capture the richness of those narratives.

One of the strengths of constructivism is its ability to reveal the nuanced realities of individuals. Researchers could study how different communities understand health, capturing the diversity of cultural beliefs through detailed ethnographic interviews. However, this focus on specificity can lead to challenges in generalising findings to broader populations.

Critical realism, on the other hand, offers a robust framework for investigating causal relationships. It encourages researchers to look beyond surface-level observations and to uncover the underlying structures that shape social phenomena. For example, a critical realist examining educational inequality could analyse how funding disparities and socio-economic status affect student outcomes. Such research helps identify the deeper social mechanisms, providing insights that can inform effective interventions.

The Value of Integration

However, the landscape of social science research is not dictated by rigid paradigms; integrating both positivist and post-positivist approaches can yield richer insights. Mixed methods research is a powerful bridge between these frameworks, allowing researchers to draw on the strengths of both qualitative and quantitative methods.

Imagine a study investigating the impact of a public health campaign. A positivist approach may assess its effectiveness by analysing pre- and post-campaign health statistics. Simultaneously, a post-positivist approach could involve interviews with community members to understand their perceptions of the campaign and its relevance. Combining these methodologies, the research measures outcomes and delves into the lived experiences that influence behaviour.

The Ongoing Need for Reflexivity and Contextual Awareness

As researchers navigate these paradigms, reflexivity remains critical. It's essential to continuously reflect on one's own biases, values, and the social contexts in which research is conducted. For instance, a researcher studying a controversial topic, such as immigration, should know how their background could shape their approach and interpretations.

This awareness helps ensure that the research process is ethical and that participants' voices are authentically represented. Moreover, understanding the **contextual factors** surrounding the research is vital. The social, cultural, political, and economic environments can significantly influence research outcomes. Acknowledging these aspects allows researchers to interpret findings within their specific settings effectively. For example, political attitudes measured in one context may differ in another due to varying historical or cultural influences.

Case Study: Future Directions in Research Methodology at Riverwood University

At Riverwood University, Dr Clara engaged in evolving research methodologies in the social sciences as she prepared to investigate the impact of community health initiatives on disadvantaged groups. She recognised that incorporating both quantitative and qualitative perspectives would enhance the rigour and relevance of her findings.

The Rise of Big Data

A significant trend influencing research methodology is the emergence of big data, referring to the volume, velocity, variety, veracity, and value of data now accessible to researchers.

Opportunities: Dr Clara identified potential in the extensive datasets available through social media interactions, public health records, and community surveys. For instance, by analysing large datasets from social media platforms, she could gauge public sentiment related to health behaviours, providing real-time insights into how communities engage with health initiatives.

Challenges: She also acknowledged the challenges in managing and interpreting vast data. The complexity of big data requires sophisticated computational tools and a sound understanding of statistical modelling techniques. Dr Clara knew the need to address data quality issues, such as missing values and biases from sourcing data primarily from specific demographic groups. Furthermore, ethical considerations regarding privacy and data security required her careful attention; safeguarding personal data was essential for maintaining trust.

Integrating Qualitative Methods

While big data provided extensive quantitative insights, Dr Clara recognised that it often lacked the depth necessary to understand human behaviour fully. This is where qualitative methods became important.

For example, after establishing a correlation between community health service usage and wellbeing statistics through quantitative analysis, Dr Clara planned to conduct in-depth interviews with community members. This qualitative component would enable her to explore how individuals interpret their interactions with health services, offering insights into their motivations, challenges, and contextual factors influencing their behaviours.

Methodological Innovations: Embracing Mixed Methods

Dr Clara adopted a mixed methods approach, combining quantitative and qualitative methodologies. This strategy allowed her to utilise the strengths of both paradigms, enhancing the overall quality of her research findings. For instance, in studying the effectiveness of a community health programme, she could initiate her work with quantitative surveys measuring health outcomes for participants, followed by qualitative interviews to uncover the experiences that influenced those outcomes. This combination provided a comprehensive perspective on the programme's impact.

Emerging Technologies: Enhancing Data Collection

Advancements in technology facilitated her research. Mobile applications and online platforms streamlined data collection and participant engagement. For example, Dr Clara considered using social media analytics to gather data on community discussions surrounding health issues, capturing trends and sentiments that could otherwise remain unexamined.

However, these innovations raised ethical questions regarding informed consent and the psychological impact of immersive technologies. Dr Clara was committed to conducting ethical reviews and ensuring participants were fully informed about their involvement.

Conclusion: A Vision for Future Research

As Dr Clara contemplated the future of research methodology, she recognised the opportunities presented by integrating various methods, big data, and emerging technologies. The evolving landscape requires researchers to be adaptable and leverage diverse approaches to enhance understanding of complex social phenomena.

Moreover, she understood that reflexivity—considering her own biases and the context of her research—was essential for ensuring ethical integrity and accuracy. Her focus on balancing quantitative and qualitative methods positioned her to contribute effectively to the field of social sciences.

Through her approach, Dr Clara aimed to establish a foundation for future research that would yield meaningful insights while respecting the intricacies of human behaviour and societal change. Her commitment to methodological rigour and ethical practices would encourage her colleagues at Riverwood University to consider this dynamic landscape of inquiry, ultimately enriching the knowledge and understanding of diverse communities.

Conclusion

In conclusion, critical reflection on the role of paradigms in shaping research is an ongoing process. There is no "best" paradigm; the appropriateness of a particular approach depends on the research question, the social phenomena under investigation, and the ethical frameworks guiding the researcher. Through continuous engagement with the assumptions and limitations of each paradigm, researchers can conduct more rigorous and impactful social science research.

The future of methodology lies in embracing the dynamic interplay between frameworks adapting to emerging technologies and data sources while ensuring ethical considerations remain at the forefront. This involves ongoing dialogue, collaboration, and commitment to research practices that are methodologically sound and socially responsible.

By integrating diverse perspectives and employing innovative methodologies, researchers can deepen their understanding of the social world and contribute meaningfully to our collective knowledge.

FINAL COMMENTS

Generalisation in Positivism

In positivist research, particularly in quantitative studies, generalisation refers to the ability to apply findings from a sample to a larger population. This process is crucial for establishing broadly applicable conclusions and predictions. For instance, researchers conducting polls before elections select large, representative samples to gauge public opinion. This approach ensures that the results reflect the views of the larger electorate. The concept of "data saturation" is relevant here; it occurs when sufficient data has been gathered to reliably represent the general trend within a population, meaning that additional data collection no longer yields new insights.

Data saturation is often achieved through rigorous sampling techniques, such as random or stratified sampling, enhancing the sample's representativeness. By collecting data from a diverse range of participants, researchers can confidently generalise their findings, informing stakeholders and decision-makers about the prevailing attitudes and behaviours of the population.

Transferability in Post-Positivism

In contrast, post-positivist research, mainly qualitative studies, emphasises the concept of transferability rather than generalisation. Transferability refers to the extent to which findings from a specific research, such as a case study, can be applied to other contexts or populations. This methodology recognises that while qualitative research may not yield statistically generalisable results, the insights gained can still hold relevance for broader groups.

For example, consider a case study on the effects of workplace bullying. Through in-depth interviews with affected individuals, qualitative researchers can uncover themes related to emotional distress, workplace relationships, and coping strategies. Although these insights are drawn from a specific group, the experiences of individuals dealing with workplace bullying can resonate with others in similar situations. Therefore, the findings can be considered transferable to the greater population as they reflect common themes and perspectives related to the subject matter.

In post-positivist research, providing rich, contextual details of the research setting and participant experiences is essential. This allows others to evaluate whether the case study's findings may apply to their own contexts. By documenting the nuances of participants' experiences, qualitative researchers contribute valuable insights that can inform broader discussions about workplace bullying and its effects.

Case Study

In my work with HIV-positive people, I recognised the significance of both positivist and post-positivist perspectives. During sessions, some of my HIV-positive clients who were prescribed antiretrovirals, which were clinically proven to be effective in managing the virus, stopped taking the medication.

This discrepancy between the clinical evidence supporting the use of antiretrovirals and the lived realities of these people prompted me to conduct an informal qualitative exploration. Through interviews, I sought to understand the reasons behind their decisions. It became apparent that the side effects of the medication were a significant factor in their decision to stop taking it. Many expressed feelings of illness that they found difficult to endure.

Conversely, the individuals who continued taking the medication reported that while they initially experienced adverse effects, these symptoms subsided after about three to four months. This insight was critical in shaping my approach to support those who had stopped their medication. By sharing this information, I encouraged them to persevere through the initial discomfort, as the side effects were likely temporary, and their bodies would eventually adjust to the medication.

This example illustrates how qualitative exploration can play a vital role in promoting adherence to lifesaving treatments. When I informed them that these effects would diminish over time, they were better equipped to manage their expectations and continue their treatment.

Overall, this experience reinforced the notion that qualitative insights can augment the understanding derived from quantitative data. While the statistical evidence confirmed the efficacy of antiretrovirals, the qualitative findings provided context and depth essential for fostering adherence among my clients in managing the difficulties associated with their treatment. By integrating both methodologies, researchers and practitioners can develop a more nuanced understanding of the factors influencing health behaviours, ultimately improving patient outcomes and supporting informed decision-making.

Conclusion

This work highlights the necessity for researchers to adopt a pluralistic approach when studying social phenomena. By recognising the value of both statistical evidence and personal narratives, we can develop more effective health interventions that address diverse populations' specific needs and concerns. This commitment to blending methodologies underscores the potential for research to inform practice, ultimately leading to better support for individuals navigating their health journeys.

My experiences have reinforced the importance of understanding positivist and post-positivist research frameworks. By valuing the insights gained from each perspective, I aim to contribute to a more nuanced dialogue in the field that embraces human behaviour's complexities and the significance of ethical, reflective research practices.

ACKNOWLEDGEMENTS

Completing this book would not have been possible without the support and contributions of several individuals.

First and foremost, I extend my deepest gratitude to my family, especially my husband, Philip, and my son, Kyle. Their unwavering belief in my ability to complete this project provided me with the motivation and encouragement I needed throughout the writing process. I am grateful for their patience and understanding during my long hours working on this manuscript.

I want to thank my friends, whose support and encouragement have sustained me throughout this journey. Their belief in my work means the world to me, and I am thankful for the camaraderie and inspiration they provide.

GLOSSARY

This glossary provides definitions of key terms used throughout the book.

Big Data: Large and complex datasets that often require advanced analytical techniques to manage and interpret, providing opportunities for new insights in social research.

Constructivism: A philosophical viewpoint that emphasises the socially constructed nature of reality and knowledge, recognising that social interactions and cultural contexts shape our understanding.

Critical Realism: A philosophical approach that acknowledges the existence of an objective reality but recognises the limitations of human perception and interpretation, focusing on uncovering the underlying structures that influence social phenomena.

Causation: The relationship between cause and effect, where one event leads to another; establishing causation requires careful control of variables and consideration of confounding factors.

Crystallisation: A process that enhances understanding by using multiple perspectives to examine data. It involves looking at the same phenomenon from different angles to provide a richer and more comprehensive interpretation.

Epistemology: The study of knowledge, including its nature, sources, and limits, which shapes how researchers understand what constitutes valid knowledge.

External Validity: The extent to which research findings can be generalised to other populations or settings beyond the specific sample studied.

Generalisability: The extent to which research findings can be applied to broader populations or settings.

Gestalt (in Research): A psychological concept asserting that the whole of an experience or phenomenon is perceived as greater than the sum of its parts. In research, gestalt emphasises understanding context and relationships, focusing on holistic experiences to uncover meaningful patterns and insights in data and human behaviour.

Hawthorne Effect: The phenomenon where individuals modify their behaviour in response to being observed, potentially impacting study outcomes

Hypothesis Testing: A statistical method used to determine the validity of a hypothesis by comparing sample data against a specific prediction or assumption. It involves formulating a null hypothesis (indicating no effect or difference) and an alternative hypothesis, then using statistical tests to assess the likelihood that the observed data would occur under the null hypothesis. The results inform whether to reject or fail to reject the null hypothesis based on a predetermined significance level.

Methodological Pluralism: A research approach that employs multiple methods or perspectives to answer a research question, combining quantitative and qualitative techniques to enhance understanding of complex social phenomena.

Methodology: The systematic approach to conducting research, encompassing the design, data collection, and analysis techniques employed in a study.

Ontology: The study of being or existence; it addresses questions related to the nature of reality and what entities exist.

Paradigm: A fundamental model or framework within which research is conducted, guiding researchers in their approach to investigating questions.

Phenomenology: A qualitative research approach that explores individuals' lived experiences and the meanings they ascribe to them. It focuses on understanding how people perceive and interpret their world through in-depth interviews or reflective methods, capturing the essence of specific experiences.

Positivism: A philosophical theory in research that asserts that knowledge is derived from empirical evidence obtained through observation, experimentation, and logical reasoning. It emphasises using scientific methods to study social phenomena and seeks to establish general laws or patterns that govern human behaviour, often advocating for objectivity and value neutrality in research.

Post-positivism: A philosophical approach that acknowledges the limitations of positivist assumptions and recognises the role of subjectivity and interpretation in research, emphasising the complexities of social phenomena.

Reflexivity: The practice of critical self-reflection on the researcher's own biases, assumptions, and positionality, which influences the research process and interpretations.

Reliability: The consistency and stability of measurement or findings; reliable results yield the same outcomes under repeated conditions.

Transferability: The extent to which research findings can be applied to other contexts or settings.

Triangulation: The use of multiple methods or data sources in a study to strengthen the validity of findings by confirming results from different perspectives.

Validity: The accuracy and truthfulness of measurement; valid research accurately represents the phenomena it aims to study.

REFERENCES

Akoglu, H. (2018). User's guide to correlation coefficients. *Turkish Journal of Emergency Medicine*, *18*(3), 91–93. https://doi.org/10.1016/J.TJEM.2018.08.001

Allen, M. (2017). Post Hoc Test: Scheffe Test. *The SAGE Encyclopedia of Communication Research Methods*, 1302–1303. https://doi.org/10.4135/9781483381411

Armstrong, R. A. (2014). When to use the Bonferroni correction. *Ophthalmic & Physiological Optics: The Journal of the British College of Ophthalmic Opticians (Optometrists)*, *34*(5), 502–508. https://doi.org/10.1111/OPO.12131

Bazen, A., Barg, F. K., & Takeshita, J. (2021). Research Techniques Made Simple: An Introduction to Qualitative Research. *Journal of Investigative Dermatology*, *141*(2), 241-247.e1. https://doi.org/10.1016/j.jid.2020.11.029

Bell, R., Warren, V., & Schmidt, R. (2022). *SAGE Research Methods Cases Part 1 The Application of Concurrent or Sequential Mixed- Methods Research Designs and Their Methodological and Application in Automotive Development*. 1–13.

Braun, V., Clarke, V., Boulton, E., Davey, L., & McEvoy, C. (2021). The online survey as a qualitative research tool. *International Journal of Social Research Methodology*, *24*(6), 641–654. https://doi.org/10.1080/13645579.2020.1805550

Buchanan, D. R. (1998). Beyond positivism: Humanistic perspectives on theory and research in health education. *Health Education Research*, *13*(3), 439–450. https://doi.org/10.1093/HER/13.3.439

Buetow, S. (2025). Emotionally Sensitive Thematic Analysis. *Qualitative Research in Psychology*, 1–18. https://doi.org/10.1080/14780887.2025.2462919

Busetto, L., Wick, W., & Gumbinger, C. (2020). How to use and assess qualitative research methods. *Neurological Research and Practice*, *2*(1). https://doi.org/10.1186/S42466-020-00059-Z

Casula, M., Rangarajan, N., & Shields, P. (2021). The potential of working hypotheses for deductive exploratory research. *Quality and Quantity*, *55*(5), 1703–1725. https://doi.org/10.1007/S11135-020-01072-9/TABLES/4

Chen, E. K. (2024). STRONG DETERMINISM. *Philosophers Imprint*, *24*(1). https://doi.org/10.3998/PHIMP.3250

Chen, S. W., Keglovits, M., Devine, M., & Stark, S. (2021). Sociodemographic Differences in Respondent Preferences for Survey Formats: Sampling Bias and Potential Threats to External Validity. *Archives of Rehabilitation Research and Clinical Translation*, *4*(1), 100175. https://doi.org/10.1016/J.ARRCT.2021.100175

Cohen, L., Manion, L., & Morrison, K. (2018). Research Design. In *Research methods in education*. Retrieved from https://www.routledge.com/Research-Methods-in-Education/Cohen-Manion-Morrison/p/book/9781138209886

Cook, C. E., Bailliard, A., Bent, J. A., Bialosky, J. E., Carlino, E., Colloca, L., ... Rossettini, G. (2023). An international consensus definition for contextual factors: findings from a nominal group technique. *Frontiers in Psychology*, *14*, 1178560. https://doi.org/10.3389/FPSYG.2023.1178560

Creaven, A. M., & Kirwan, E. M. (2024). Open qualitative data: a worked example of qualitative data sharing from an interview study on loneliness in young adulthood. *Qualitative Research in Psychology*. https://doi.org/10.1080/14780887.2024.2423923

Dawadi, S., Shrestha, S., & Giri, R. A. (2021). Mixed-Methods Research: A Discussion on its Types, Challenges, and Criticisms. *Journal of Practical Studies in Education*, *2*(2), 25–36. https://doi.org/10.46809/JPSE.V2I2.20

De Vos, A. S., Strydom, H., Fouche, C. B., & Delport, C. S. L. (2005). Research at grass roots. Pretoria. *Government Printers*, *2021*, 1–521. Retrieved from https://search.worldcat.org/title/1232458705

Delmas, P. M., & Giles, R. L. (2022). Qualitative research approaches and their application in education. *International Encyclopedia of Education: Fourth Edition*, 24–32. https://doi.org/10.1016/B978-0-12-818630-5.11003-6

Denicolo, P., Long, T., & Bradley-Cole, K. (2016). Linking philosophy and theory to research purpose.

Constructivist Approaches and Research Methods: A Practical Guide to Exploring Personal Meanings, 25–38. https://doi.org/10.4135/9781526402660

Denzin, N. K., & Lincoln, Y. S. (2004). *The Sage handbook of qualitative research [El manual SAGE de investigación cualitativa]*. 968.

Edmonds, W. A., & Kennedy, T. D. (2017). Explanatory-Sequential Approach. *An Applied Guide to Research Designs: Quantitative, Qualitative, and Mixed Methods*, 196–200. https://doi.org/10.4135/9781071802779

Ellingson, L. L. (2017). Crystallization. *The International Encyclopedia of Communication Research Methods*, 1–5. https://doi.org/10.1002/9781118901731.IECRM0055

Figueiredo, M., Eloy, S., Marques, S., & Dias, L. (2023). Older people perceptions on the built environment: A scoping review. *Applied Ergonomics, 108*. https://doi.org/10.1016/j.apergo.2022.103951

Fletcher, A. J. (2017). Applying critical realism in qualitative research: methodology meets method. *International Journal of Social Research Methodology, 20*(2), 181–194. https://doi.org/10.1080/13645579.2016.1144401

Fodouop Kouam, A. W. (2024). Interpretivism or Constructivism: Navigating Research Paradigms in Social Science Research. *International Journal of Research Publications, 143*(1).

Gabriel, M. (2015). *Fields of Sense: A New Realist Ontology (Speculative Realism EUP)*. Retrieved from http://www.amazon.com/exec/obidos/redirect?tag=citeulike07-20&path=ASIN/0748692894

Gaillet, L. L. (2012). (Per)forming archival research methodologies. *College Composition and Communication, 64*(1), 35–58. https://doi.org/10.58680/CCC201220858/CITE/REFWORKS

García Portilla, J. (2022). Research Setting. *Contributions to Economics*, 13–17. https://doi.org/10.1007/978-3-030-78498-0_2

Gillespie, R. (2003). *Manufacturing knowledge: a history of the Hawthorne experiments*. 282.

Gordon, R. A. (2015). Regression analysis for the social sciences: Second edition. *Regression Analysis for the Social Sciences: Second Edition*, 1–543. https://doi.org/10.4324/9781315748788

Gwet, K. L. (2014). 2.5 The Kappa coefficient and Its Paradoxes. *Handbook of Inter-Rater Reliability: The Definitive Guide to Measuring the Extent of Agreement among Raters*, 57–62.

Hammersley, M. (2017). On the role of values in social research: Weber vindicated? *Sociological Research Online, 22*(1). https://doi.org/10.5153/SRO.4197

Handley, M. A., Lyles, C. R., McCulloch, C., & Cattamanchi, A. (2018). Selecting and Improving Quasi-Experimental Designs in Effectiveness and Implementation Research. *Annual Review of Public Health, 39*, 5. https://doi.org/10.1146/ANNUREV-PUBLHEALTH-040617-014128

Hariton, E., & Locascio, J. J. (2018). Randomised controlled trials—the gold standard for effectiveness research. *BJOG: An International Journal of Obstetrics and Gynaecology, 125*(13), 1716. https://doi.org/10.1111/1471-0528.15199

Hawthorne Effect Definition: How It Works and Is It Real. (n.d.). Retrieved February 11, 2025, from The Hawthorne Effect Handbook - Everything You Need To Know About Hawthorne Effect website: https://www.investopedia.com/terms/h/hawthorne-effect.asp

Heale, R., & Twycross, A. (2015). Validity and reliability in quantitative studies. *Evidence-Based Nursing, 18*(3), 66–67. https://doi.org/10.1136/EB-2015-102129

Horowitz, I. L. (2004). Two cultures of science: The limits of positivism. *International Social Science Journal, 56*(181), 429–437. https://doi.org/10.1111/J.0020-8701.2004.00504.X

Huesemann, M. H. (2002). The inherent biases in environmental research and their effects on public policy. *Futures, 34*(7), 621–633. https://doi.org/10.1016/S0016-3287(02)00004-6

John', S., Labrador, C., Younas, A., & Ali, P. (2021). Understanding and interpreting regression analysis. *Evidence-Based Nursing, 24*(4), 116–118. https://doi.org/10.1136/EBNURS-2021-103425

Kaufman, C. E., & Ramarao, S. (2005). Community confidentiality, consent, and the individual research process: Implications for demographic research. *Population Research and Policy Review, 24*(2), 149–173. https://doi.org/10.1007/S11113-004-0329-9/METRICS

Keyter, A., & Roos, V. (2015). MENTAL HEALTH WORKERS' COPING STRATEGIES IN DEALING WITH CONTINUOUS SECONDARY TRAUMA. *Southern African Journal of Social Work and Social Development, 27*(3), 365–382. https://doi.org/10.25159/2415-5829/724

Kim, H.-Y. (2014a). Analysis of variance (ANOVA) comparing means of more than two groups. *Restorative Dentistry & Endodontics, 39*(1), 74. https://doi.org/10.5395/RDE.2014.39.1.74

Kim, H.-Y. (2014b). Analysis of variance (ANOVA) comparing means of more than two groups. *Restorative Dentistry & Endodontics, 39*(1), 74. https://doi.org/10.5395/RDE.2014.39.1.74

Korstjens, I., & Moser, A. (2017). Series: Practical guidance to qualitative research. Part 4: Trustworthiness and publishing. *The European Journal of General Practice, 24*(1), 120. https://doi.org/10.1080/13814788.2017.1375092

Kramer, M. W., & Adams, T. E. (2017). Ethnography. *The SAGE Encyclopedia of Communication Research Methods*, 458–461. https://doi.org/10.4135/9781483381411

Lane, D. M. (2010). Tukey's Honestly Significant Difference (HSD). *Encyclopedia of Research Design*, 1566–1570. https://doi.org/10.4135/9781412961288

Lexchin, J. (2012). Sponsorship bias in clinical research. *The International Journal of Risk & Safety in Medicine*, 24(4), 233–242. https://doi.org/10.3233/JRS-2012-0574

Lobmeier, J. H. (2010). Nonexperimental Designs. *Encyclopedia of Research Design*, 911–914. https://doi.org/10.4135/9781412961288

Mahtani, K., Spencer, E. A., Brassey, J., & Heneghan, C. (2018). Catalogue of bias: observer bias. *BMJ Evidence-Based Medicine*, 23(1), 23–24. https://doi.org/10.1136/EBMED-2017-110884

Maksimović, J., & Evtimov, J. (2023). Positivism and post-positivism as the basis of quantitative research in pedagogy. *Research in Pedagogy*, 13(1), 208–218. https://doi.org/10.5937/ISTRPED2301208M

Matilda, S. (2016). Big data in social media environment: A business perspective. *Social Media Listening and Monitoring for Business Applications*, 70–93. https://doi.org/10.4018/978-1-5225-0846-5.CH004

McCambridge, J., Witton, J., & Elbourne, D. R. (2014). Systematic review of the Hawthorne effect: New concepts are needed to study research participation effects. *Journal of Clinical Epidemiology*, 67(3), 267. https://doi.org/10.1016/J.JCLINEPI.2013.08.015

Mishra, P., Singh, U., Pandey, C. M., Mishra, P., & Pandey, G. (2019). Application of Student's t-test, Analysis of Variance, and Covariance. *Annals of Cardiac Anaesthesia*, 22(4), 407. https://doi.org/10.4103/ACA.ACA_94_19

Mishra, S., & Datta-Gupta, A. (2018). Experimental Design and Response Surface Analysis. *Applied Statistical Modeling and Data Analytics*, 169–193. https://doi.org/10.1016/B978-0-12-803279-4.00007-9

Monaghan, T. F., Agudelo, C. W., Rahman, S. N., Wein, A. J., Lazar, J. M., Everaert, K., & Dmochowski, R. R. (2021). Blinding in Clinical Trials: Seeing the Big Picture. *Medicina*, 57(7), 647. https://doi.org/10.3390/MEDICINA57070647

Pampel, F. C., Krueger, P. M., & Denney, J. T. (2010). Socioeconomic Disparities in Health Behaviors. *Annual Review of Sociology*, 36, 349. https://doi.org/10.1146/ANNUREV.SOC.012809.102529

Parsons, H. M. (1974). What Happened at Hawthorne? *Science*, 183(4128), 922–932. https://doi.org/10.1126/SCIENCE.183.4128.922

Patino, C. M., & Ferreira, J. C. (2018). Internal and external validity: can you apply research study results to your patients? *Jornal Brasileiro de Pneumologia*, 44(3), 183. https://doi.org/10.1590/S1806-37562018000000164

Patton, M. Q. (1999). Enhancing the quality and credibility of qualitative analysis. *Health Services Research*, 34(5 Pt 2), 1189. Retrieved from https://pmc.ncbi.nlm.nih.gov/articles/PMC1089059/

Positivism | Definition, History, Theories, & Criticism | Britannica. (n.d.). Retrieved February 11, 2025, from https://www.britannica.com/topic/positivism

Revicki, D. (2014). Internal Consistency Reliability. *Encyclopedia of Quality of Life and Well-Being Research*, 3305–3306. https://doi.org/10.1007/978-94-007-0753-5_1494

Roos, V., van der Westhuizen, J., & Keyter, A. (2016). Participants' reflections on participating in the Mmogo-method: The example of mental health workers' coping strategies. *Understanding Relational and Group Experiences Through the Mmogo-Method*, 215–227. https://doi.org/10.1007/978-3-319-31224-8_11

Rutkowski, D., Rutkowski, L., Thompson, G., & Canbolat, Y. (2024). The limits of inference: reassessing causality in international assessments. *Large-Scale Assessments in Education*, 12(1), 1–18. https://doi.org/10.1186/S40536-024-00197-9/FIGURES/1

Saeed, N., & Husamaldin, L. (2021). Big Data Characteristics (V's) in Industry. *Iraqi Journal of Industrial Research*, 8(1), 1–9. https://doi.org/10.53523/IJOIRVOL8I1ID52

Sapsford, R. (2007). *Survey research*. 276.

Schweizer, M. L., Braun, B. I., & Milstone, A. M. (2016). Research Methods in Healthcare Epidemiology and Antimicrobial Stewardship – Quasi-Experimental Designs. *Infection Control and Hospital Epidemiology*, 37(10), 1135. https://doi.org/10.1017/ICE.2016.117

Shannon-Baker, P. (2023). Philosophical underpinnings of mixed methods research in education. *International Encyclopedia of Education(Fourth Edition)*, 380–389. https://doi.org/10.1016/B978-0-12-818630-5.11037-1

Shin, Y. (2017). *Time series analysis in the social sciences: the fundamentals*. 232.

Shiyanbola, O. O., Rao, D., Bolt, D., Brown, C., Zhang, M., & Ward, E. (2021). Using an exploratory sequential mixed methods design to adapt an Illness Perception Questionnaire for African Americans with diabetes: the mixed data integration process. *Health Psychology and Behavioral Medicine*, 9(1), 796. https://doi.org/10.1080/21642850.2021.1976650

Sibbald, B., & Roland, M. (1998). Understanding controlled trials. Why are randomised controlled trials important? *BMJ: British Medical Journal*, *316*(7126), 201. https://doi.org/10.1136/BMJ.316.7126.201

Smirnov, E. (2024). Enhancing qualitative research in psychology with large language models: a methodological exploration and examples of simulations. *Qualitative Research in Psychology*. https://doi.org/10.1080/14780887.2024.2428255

Sovacool, B. K., Axsen, J., & Sorrell, S. (2018). Promoting novelty, rigor, and style in energy social science: Towards codes of practice for appropriate methods and research design. *Energy Research and Social Science*, *45*, 12–42. https://doi.org/10.1016/j.erss.2018.07.007

Spiliopoulos, L., & Hertwig, R. (2024). Stochastic heuristics for decisions under risk and uncertainty. *Frontiers in Psychology*, *15*. https://doi.org/10.3389/FPSYG.2024.1438581/FULL

Stern, C., Lizarondo, L., Carrier, J., Godfrey, C., Rieger, K., Salmond, S., ... Loveday, H. (2020). Methodological guidance for the conduct of mixed methods systematic reviews. *JBI Evidence Synthesis*, *18*(10), 2108–2118. https://doi.org/10.11124/JBISRIR-D-19-00169

Suzuki, M., & Yamamoto, Y. (2021). Characterizing the Influence of Confirmation Bias on Web Search Behavior. *Frontiers in Psychology*, *12*. https://doi.org/10.3389/FPSYG.2021.771948/FULL

Swift, A. (2022). Being Creative with Resources in Qualitative Research. *The SAGE Handbook of Qualitative Research Design*, 290–306. https://doi.org/10.4135/9781529770278.N19

Syed Mohammad, A. N. (2009). (PDF) Factor Analysis: Nature, Mechanism & Uses in Social and Management Researches. Retrieved February 16, 2025, from Journal of Cost and Management Accountant website: https://www.researchgate.net/publication/200564629_Factor_Analysis_Nature_Mechanism_Uses_in_Social_and_Management_Researches

Thakkar, J. J. (2020). *Structural Equation Modelling*. *285*. https://doi.org/10.1007/978-981-15-3793-6

Tiokhin, L., Hackman, J., Munira, S., Jesmin, K., & Hruschka, D. (2019). Generalizability is not optional: insights from a cross-cultural study of social discounting. *Royal Society Open Science*, *6*(2). https://doi.org/10.1098/RSOS.181386

Vilagut, G. (2014). Test-Retest Reliability. *Encyclopedia of Quality of Life and Well-Being Research*, 6622–6625. https://doi.org/10.1007/978-94-007-0753-5_3001

Wang, C., Chen, M. H., Schifano, E., Wu, J., & Yan, J. (2016). Statistical methods and computing for big data. *Statistics and Its Interface*, *9*(4), 399. https://doi.org/10.4310/SII.2016.V9.N4.A1

Watkins, E. R., & Newbold, A. (2020). Factorial Designs Help to Understand How Psychological Therapy Works. *Frontiers in Psychiatry*, *11*, 429. https://doi.org/10.3389/FPSYT.2020.00429

Yeager, K. (n.d.). *LibGuides: SPSS Tutorials: Chi-Square Test of Independence*. Retrieved from https://libguides.library.kent.edu/SPSS/ChiSquare

AUTHOR BIOGRAPHY

Anna Tierney née Keyter, is a dedicated research psychologist and psychotherapist originally from New Zealand, now based in Hull, UK. She holds an MA degree in Research Psychology, an MSc in Rehabilitation Psychology, and various MA certificates in Psychotherapy. Since 2017, Anna has successfully run her own counselling practice, Online Therapy NZ, providing services and support to clients. She has been practicing as a counsellor since 2004 and has also worked with not-for-profit organisations to support those less fortunate.

Anna's research interests focus on the intersection of psychological practice and empirical research, where she aims to bridge the gap between theory and practice. She has several publications and is committed to advancing knowledge in the field.

---

[1] While 0.05 is a widely used threshold, it is important to note that it is not a rigid rule. Researchers may choose different alpha levels based on the context of their study, the consequences of errors, and specific field standards. Additionally, there is an increasing trend towards reporting p-values as continuous measures rather than strictly adhering to the 0.05 cutoff, allowing for a more nuanced interpretation of results.

www.ingramcontent.com/pod-product-compliance
Lightning Source LLC
Chambersburg PA
CBHW081359270326
41930CB00015B/3359